What Others are Saying about t

Eric Hogue is one of the best! He has mastered his craft and is one of the few that are leading and doing it the right way. Many organizations see givers as money machines and the Fundraiser's job to separate the donor from their money. Eric sees donors as stewards of the resources they have and his job to help them steward their resources well. *The Winning Side of "the Ask"* is bound to become a valuable asset for anyone starting in fundraising and anyone who Is not entirely sure how to be successful at their job of fundraising. If you're young in the profession, it's a road map of how to be successful. If you're a CEO of a non-profit, it's an excellent resource for you to understand the work of your development team and how you can work with them to support your mission and vision. I anticipate this to become one of the must-reads for every fundraising shop everywhere.

Bruce Scott
Senior Vice President of Business Development
Westfall Gold

In *The Winning Side of "the Ask"* Eric Hogue shows us how to build sustainable fundraising practices on bedrock values, how to develop a vocabulary and nomenclature consistent with those values, how to organize and weigh a highly functional and adaptive advancement operation, and how to engage prospects and donors in respectful, graceful and meaningful ways to create lasting, difference-making philanthropic compacts. His observations are honest, his critiques sound and his practical advice immensely helpful. *The Winning Side of "the Ask"* is a valuable addition to our storehouse of enlightened, applicable, forward-leading advancement texts.

Jim Langley
President, Langley Innovations

My bookshelves are filled with fundraising books that contain tips for capitalizing on campaign strategies, increasing donations or developing effective advancement teams, but *The Winning Side of "the Ask"* is a one-stop shop for fundraising professionals. Eric masterfully explains the principles and practices of donor-centric fundraising through anecdotal examples and first-hand experiences that make his content immediately applicable. From how to become a better listener, earn trust with donors, and prepare for an ask – Eric answers the most commonly asked questions in philanthropy, providing readers with both the *why* and the *how*. Every Fundraiser looking to make a *lasting* impact on their organization should get their hands on this book and heed the words that come from one of the best donor-centric Fundraisers I know.

Dr. Andrew Flamm
President, Grace College and Seminary

Eric Hogue has gifted NPOs with *The Winning Side of "the Ask"*, a masterpiece of relevant theory and practices that reflect what Jesus modeled in His relationships. Eric writes with knowledge born of rich experience, a passion for his craft, and a love for God and people. With profound simplicity, Eric expresses the way in which each of us prefers and appreciates to be invited into the philanthropic process. Whether you are a rookie or veteran to the calling and ministry of philanthropic advising, Eric's acumens provide luscious morsels of professional development. His insights and pertinent data are also applicable, actionable, and beneficial to leaders in any capacity. Even as he provides a model of donor-centric fundraising, he demonstrates visionary leadership that transforms old perceptions of organizational constituents. Thank you for being God's man in God's place for such a time as this, Eric. Your life is a gift.

Dr. Carol Summers
Professor of Education Emeritus, Olivet Nazarene University

The Winning Side of "the Ask" will become your manual for serving your donors and your cause. When passion intersects with trust is where giving is maximized. Eric Hogue helps us to identify passions and increase trust so that we see great fundraising success. Our team will be reading this book every year!

Dr. John Jackson
President, Jessup University

By reading *The Winning Side of "the Ask"*, you will discover what I already know. Eric Hogue is a creative and entrepreneurial voice to the fund-raising world. His focus on donor centric philanthropy and authentic, relational fundraising is exactly what Christian non-profits need to hear. Follow his lead, and your job will be changed forever. Follow his lead and your non-profit will grow its impact in the mission field. Follow his lead and your donors will never see you the same again. Thanks Eric, for offering us a prophetic call to action. May we all have ears to hear and hearts to serve.

Richard Blackmon
Principal; CEO, The Giving Crowd

With candor and humility, Eric Hogue shares his own story of growing into a donor-centric frame of fundraising while sprinkling in many examples of others who have entered the fundraising profession and learned hard but valuable lessons. Reading *The Winning Side of "the Ask"* will give both the seasoned and beginning fundraising professional guidance and courage to go beyond the well-worn path of ordinary fundraising to the narrower path to fundraising excellence. Ignore these lessons to your professional peril!

R. Mark Dillon, PhD
Senior VP and Founder, Total Advancement Solutions

Not often can you say that you were there with someone at the beginning of their journey. I had that privilege with Eric Hogue. It became clear very quickly that this new philanthropy role wasn't just a job for him but a calling. In *The Winning Side of "the Ask"*, Eric shares not just practical advice for advancing a cause but the integrity in the journey that makes all the difference. His years as a non-profit higher education leader allow Eric to provide invaluable insights when your mission is your cause. He shares real situations that professionals can relate to as they achieve those famous "fund-raising goals." It always has been about the donor and their connection to the need. Eric Hogue understands that and can help you embrace it with tried-and-true methods and lessons learned.

Dr. Rhonda Allison Capron
Retired Vice Chancellor and Dean

The Winning Side of "The Ask"

Eric K. Hogue, MATS

FaithHappenings Publishing

Centennial, Colo

All Scripture quotations are from the English Standard Version (ESV) published by Crossway Publishers, 2015. Used by permission.

For bulk orders, please contact the publisher at:

FaithHappenings Publishing
A division of WordServe Literary
7500 E. Arapahoe Rd. Suite 285
Centennial, CO 80112
admin@wordserveliterary.com
303.471.6675

Cover Design: Tehsin Gul

Interior Book Design: Greg Johnson

Eric Hogue, 1964

ISBN: 978-1-941555-57-6

Printed in the United States of America

Contents

Dedication

I *cultivated* enough nerve to make '*the ask*' and she accepted – and then, on December 17, 1988, the *pledged commitment* was fulfilled before God, family, and friends.

Now, some 34-plus years later, Tammy continues to be the love of my life and my best friend. I am personally, professionally, and eternally grateful for her, our two brilliant daughters, stellar sons-in-law, three amazing grandchildren, and our extended family for their constant love and cheer filled encouragement.

I thank God for "*The Hogue Hut.*"

Eric

Introduction

"I'm convinced that people aren't giving as much because the process of giving is fundamentally flawed, unproductive, and often downright unpleasant."

-- Lisa Greer *"Philanthropy Revolution"*

What comes to mind when you hear the word "Fundraiser?" (And I'll be capitalizing this word throughout this book when I refer to the person or the vocation of Fundraising.)

Does it imply an easy and simplistic job? You just ask for money from wealthy people, right? The reality is so much more complex. To cultivate a *donor-centric* relationship — with intentionally philanthropic individuals . . . is much harder. It takes time and personal investment to build and cultivate philanthropic relationships. To raise money as a profession is tremendously difficult but when it is done right, it is one of life's most rewarding vocations.

Like many things in life, there is a right way and a wrong way to go about Fundraising. One method, the "donor-centric method," will lead to *sustainable* success.

My intent is to explain, describe, and prescribe an authentic donor-centric method in the following pages of this book.

If you have the stamina and determination to learn how to be donor-centric and develop specific systems and processes, you will never work another day in your life. You will go to work but never call it "work." Instead, you will call it "opportunity."

But if you grow lazy on the personal processes or learning the different and appropriate systems of Fundraising, you will become deeply frustrated in about eighteen months. You will eventually hate this good work and look to leave it, never to return again. It all comes down to you performing the work correctly for the right reasons and through the right lens, versus you simply doing the work wantonly for a paycheck.

Through my fifteen-plus years in this vocation, I have learned that looking ahead and building your skill set is one of the key aspects to success. As you listen to donors – *I mean really listen to them* – you will increase your ability to move beyond just asking for a donation. Instead, you will come alongside your donors and help them achieve what they want to do with their God-given provisions. As you work with your donors, they will grow to trust you and listen to you because you have proven yourself to be a valued "philanthropic advisor." Eventually, your donors will not make any donations to any nonprofit organization or cause without first speaking with you.

Through the years, I've known many people who have gone into this profession. On the surface, they looked like they would be stellar at Fundraising yet they only lasted eighteen to twenty months. These people did what they "thought" they should be doing instead of taking a narrower path. In this book, I will teach you how to follow a distinct path of philanthropy; one that will lead to success, for your donors first, and for you as a donor-centric Fundraiser.

The Donor Hoarder

When I arrived at Colorado Christian University, the Office of University Advancement had been dormant for nearly two years. The staff had dwindled to three full-time staff members. I walked into my first staff meeting with Sarah and discovered a delightful person with a big heart. From our first interaction, Sarah clearly loved the university and its very distinct and compelling Christ-centered liberal arts higher education mission. Sarah, holding the title and role as a Major Gift Officer, held many of the university's top donors in her portfolio.

I asked her, "How many donors are your responsibility?"

"Six hundred and eighty," she responded without a hint of regret or hesitation.

I was stunned with her answer . . . yet not surprised. We were a small shop and Sarah had every intention to be successful with her large group of self-assigned donors. When I heard this number, I began to do the math. Even if Sarah reached out to one or two donors every day of the year, she would never build the necessary *authentic connections* needed to be successful.

Sarah felt that she was forced into being a "donor hoarder."

It was impossible for her to engage with them in a fruitful and consistent manner. It is impractical for one person to build relationships of trust with 680 individuals and philanthropic households. As we talked, I learned Sarah's portfolio contained new donors, prospective donors, major donors, and tenured donors (donors who were new to the university, prospects for future gifts, and confirmed major donors). Her portfolio was a potpourri of uncultivated donors.

"Are you completing your donor contact reports?" I asked.

Sarah's face grew a tint of red and she admitted, "No, Eric, it's been hard being the only active gift officer in our department."

I wasn't surprised by her answer and had already noticed a shortage of donor contact reports in the files of my department.

Sarah's strategy for fundraising was something I call "hope, spray, and pray." She operated this large portfolio of names hoping to simply raise money by making friends. I am not a believer in the often-used phrase philosophy that "friend making is Fundraising." Building intentionally donor-centric relationships is a Fundraising relationship and not simply friend making. Believe me, today's donors know the difference, and they search for philanthropic professionals who operate in this manner. It was little wonder Sarah was overwhelmed with her responsibilities.

Ideally, the typical Major Gift Officer (MGO) at most donor dependent institutions is responsible for seventy-five to 100 individuals. It's a far more manageable number for building productive and meaningful relationships throughout the year. With this ratio as a rule, Sarah could have encouraged the administration to hire additional MGOs versus holding onto 680 donors to cultivate by herself. For example, 400 donors assigned equally to four intentional gift officers would have much more success, sustainability, and better futures for the mission of the nonprofit for years to come.

I discussed this flippant "friend-making" philosophy with an experienced consultant who operates a successful consulting firm in Denver, Colorado. Scott Lumpkin, of Lumpkin Associates said, "Legitimate and well-organized donor portfolios are the biggest barrier for successful fundraising results for 80% of the nonprofits, ministries and organizations in Colorado." If you believe a large portfolio is the way to raise a lot of money, it is not. If you don't learn what a donor-centric portfolio needs to be, then you will stay in the muck and mire of a massive donor portfolio and find yourself burned out, stressed out, and employing desperate measures within eighteen months.

Later in these pages, I will include a chapter that discusses best practices for a "right-sized" donor portfolio for your mission, your donors, and you – the Fundraiser.

The Unrealistic, Unrestricted Campaign

Stephen recently became a vice president at a nonprofit organization. He called me one Monday, and as I listened to his story, I could hear the stress level rising in his voice to almost the panic level. He began, "My CEO, Henry, called me into his office and then told me about a capital campaign we needed to run. His new boss said, 'Your department needs to raise $11 million this season to satisfy our board and meet our growing operational needs.' "

There was no research or specific reason behind setting such a campaign goal.

"Stephen," I said with empathy. "You are in a really difficult situation. We both know no donor is passionate when they hear about a nonprofit's fundraising campaign goal designated strictly to their annual operational budget and undescribed needs. I know this situation is especially true when you work for a revenue producing organization like I do, where the university has operational revenue streams including tuition, room and board, or miscellaneous fees. Raising money for an operational budget while receiving product-significant revenue streams is a sure way to reduce your donor roster. Donors want to make an impact with their gift that delivers a measurable outcome. They do not want to give their gifts to compounding annual debt of the organization's operations.

Stephen faced a recurring and systemic problem within his organization. Every nonprofit director or president would love to sit in their office and create unaccountable, unrestricted annual fundraising goals. Stephen will have to use a bit of diplomacy as he speaks some truth to his new CEO, Henry. Instead of pulling a fundraising number out of the air and assigning it to Stephen and his staff, if Henry believes his fundraising request to be legitimate, he should have asked, "Stephen, what do you think your staff can raise this year for operations?" Or even better, "Do you think we can raise more money this year than last year and assign a portion of the year-over-year raise margin to operations?"

A warning here: when Stephen receives these types of questions from CEO Henry, he should not answer right away. It's better for Stephen to say, "Let me do some research, talk with my team and get back to you." If Henry had gone this route with his unrestricted fiscal campaign request, he gives Stephen the ability to work with his trained colleagues, gather some plausible fundraising projections and then return to the CEO with a much stronger and realistic fundraising strategy. This revised plan also gives Stephen and the other gift officers the chance to personally speak with their donors and find out what they think about the campaign, how they feel about giving unrestricted donations, and what each donor might want to do in helping the current situation.

In a return meeting, Stephen could then present to Henry, his CEO, the following: "I talked with my gift officers and a number of our donors are willing to give unrestrictedly, but they are really interested in restricting their gifts this year to our projects and missional outcomes. Actually, a strategic and diversified comprehensive campaign this year might be much more donor-centric because of what the organization is going through and where it needs to go in the future with philanthropy."

Numerous times I have experienced poor results when the CEO, president, or executive director makes top-down fundraising mandates to the vice president or the director of development. It's like he or she takes a horse whip to his staff to meet the unresearched goal. Then the director mandates the staff, and the staff pushes their donors to meet the goal, instead of being donor-centric and listening to what the donor wants to do to help the organization grow and meet its missional purpose(s). Certainly, Stephen and Henry will raise some funds and get a few large, one-time gifts, but the process will turn away many donors and eventually lead to donor apathy. This result forces gift officers into a frantic performance in front of their donors which is an immediate turn off. The long-term result is they never hit their future goals. In turn, without some serious intervention, Stephen will grow more and more frustrated and unsuccessful with this top-down fundraising mandate from his CEO. After eighteen months, Stephen will be looking for the exit and a different job.

There is a way to work with your colleagues in both a small shop and a large shop where your projections for fundraising are collegial and authentic and not just "hopeful, spray and pray" goals. Even in a small shop with perhaps you and a director, there has to be an established trust and transparent communications where you can set an appropriate fundraising goal for the year. The secret sauce is including the donors. Donors want to partner with you in determining their favorite nonprofit's fundraising campaigns. This is only accomplished if you have built a sincerely donor-centric style of fundraising that features outcomes and impacts versus the organizational needs.

In the manipulated top-down fundraising style, the gift officers will frenetically default to donor leveraging rhetoric by saying, "Let me go out and find a whale (or a very rich person with a lot of money to give). Or they will do a Hail Mary pass and ask, "Who are my top five donors?" Let's go out and ring them up." Or "Let's make the big ask to our most loyal donor and drop the hammer." They may guilt the donor enough that they will get some money. But this donor will not give again, because for the donor, that experience was not enjoyable or rewarding. In the majority of cases this type of cultivation practice will burn the relationship.

I often repeat the phrase, "Desperate people do and say desperate things." The only way to not be desperate as a Fundraiser is to be strategic, authentic, and to know what you are doing —and why! You also need the ability to teach others in your organization what you are doing in order to be successful as a Fundraiser. Further, it's imperative to interact respectfully, speak the truth to power, and explain to your boss why all these systems and processes of equity and time are going to be invested into these donor relationships. It is because in the end, it produces a fruitful donor relationship.

Top-down projections and goals are not philanthropy, but self-centered philanthropic myopia. This book will detail processes, systems and skill sets that will enable you to become successful in charting year-to-year donor-centric fundraising projections.

Fundraising Requires More Than Writing Ability

Appeal letters and various written communication pieces are fundamental tools for small shops and nonprofits. Throughout the year, fundraising departments will send three or four appeal letters to raise funds for their organization. For smaller shops, operational funds are important, and the appeal letters raise the necessary funds.

Roger Harrison loves to write, and he took a job with a nonprofit in downtown Chicago. In a meeting with his director Jason, Roger informed him, "I love to write and tell stories." The director immediately assigned Roger to write the nonprofit donor appeal letters.

Roger poured his love of writing into his work on these periodic appeal letters. He would often write a 5,000-word letter and send it to the entire donor base. Year after year these appeal letters fell short of raising the needed funds. As a writer, Roger became increasingly frustrated and at times knew his well-written prose wasn't having the impact everyone wanted.

Roger's appeal letters were usually written in the second or third person and offered many giving options about the various needs of the nonprofit instead of a specific opportunity or offer. When the response didn't meet anyone's expectations, he put more money into the letter campaigns and upscaled the look and feel of the mailings with high-quality paper and elaborately colored envelopes. With each addition, the cost of each appeal letter eventually rose from $1.25 to $4.10! Roger believed if he spent more money on the appeal letter, maybe it would achieve better results. Yet Roger continued to craft and write each appeal letter as if it were a novella. The problem: His strategy and process for writing appeal letters was not employing the right methodology.

An appeal letter should never be written in third person. It must be written in first person and directed to a single individual and not a group of people or posed in a plural form. The word "you" must be used – *frequently through the letter*. The letter must speak from the perspective of the appeal letter's author. The letter rarely needs to be five pages but can be a single page or a page and a half. It needs to express the need to the donor in a distinct, clear, and attainable manner. In addition, the offer needs to have several different gift amounts depending on the giving ability of each donor segmentation. Each of these details are essential elements in writing appeal letters, but Roger never took the time to learn these vital processes to write a winning appeal letter. Later in this book, I will offer you sound instruction on how to write a successful appeal letter. I promise, if you use these proven donor-centric practices, even writing a one-or two-page appeal letter can completely turn around the philanthropic results for your nonprofit.

When I started out in fundraising, I thought a four-page appeal letter would cover all the bases. Then I realized that donors read the mail file variable data at the top of the letter. They quickly skim the initial paragraph — sometimes just the initial sentence. After these two quick views the donors begin to look for the donor opportunity or offer. Finally, they flip the one-page letter over and look for the signature and any postscript message. Experience tells me that this "1, 2, 3, 4 scenario" is what donors initially read in any appeal letter. Well-written appeal letters don't use flowery words and they repeat the offer three times in the letter. Understanding these proven details and communicating appropriately in them will raise the response rate from fifty- to sixty-percent. If you follow these practices, you previously may have had one person out of ten letters respond to your offer, but utilizing my prescribed appeal letter strategies, you will increase that ratio to four, or five donors out of ten responding with a generous donation via your appeal letter campaign.

The Gerrymandered Capital Campaign

Larry Smith worked at a small Christian college and was offered a job at another larger Christian university. He took the leap. In the new job, Larry was moving up from a university gift officer position to vice president at his new assignment. While excited about this new job, he also had some concerns because his work would be changing and expanding. Instead of tending to the 125-donor portfolio, Larry was now going to have to manage a fundraising team while determining a strategy for each fundraising campaign. He still had a donor portfolio, but upon starting in the new role, he began to work with the president and dove into an immediate capital campaign.

In his first phone call to me, Larry asked, "Eric, how should I organize my staff meetings? How do I continue my focus on my portfolio and orchestrate portfolio meetings for my gift officers?" We went through the process of who should be in the staff meeting, and we discussed a portfolio meeting and the appropriate agendas for this group of staff members. Our discussion was basic logistics. Larry understood his job was changing. As a part of managing people, he had to cast vision, create strategy, develop a process toward success, and inspect what he expected from his team of professionals.

Unexpectedly, the president asked Larry to create an $80 million capital campaign with his staff of eleven which included four major gift officers.

Larry's first question was, "What is this capital campaign's case statement and case for support?"

The president said, "Look, we need to build a new building. We need to renovate the old building. We need some new athletic fields, and we need to buy the available property right across the street of campus."

Larry said, "That's fantastic. What type of research have we put into determining that this is the right thing to do?"

The president said, "Well, it fits our mission. Our growth is demanding it. I want to do this, and the board wants to do it. We believe we can raise the $80 million within seven years and make this campaign a success."

After the initial conversation with his president, Larry returned to his office totally frustrated. He called me and told me the details of the request. I was excited he was now a vice president and had the opportunity to build and strategize with his team. Plus, he was going to determine how they were going to communicate their message and get donors excited. He was on a path to launch a successful campaign.

Then I asked two questions, "What did your feasibility study instrument say?"

"We didn't do a feasibility study," he said.

Then I asked, "OK ... well, what does your top donor base have to say?"

"I don't think the capacity is there," he said with a shrug of his shoulders.

"Then you have asked them?"

"No," he said. "I can tell by simply researching the database, the donor capacity we need for a campaign of this magnitude is not there."

I pressed further. "You will need to request a sincere feasibility study." A feasibility study is when you survey about forty to sixty lead donors who are close partners and believe in your mission. Then you ask them a series of questions about what *they* think the organization needs to do to move the mission's outcome and impact forward. This process can work for any nonprofit, mission, or church.

If you ask the donor, at the end of the questionnaire instrument, they will tell you if they can help with the campaign and its projected goal. In Larry's case, there was no feasibility study and there wasn't time to perform one in the near future.

I call Larry's situation the *"gerrymander capital campaign"* where the leadership of a church, mission, university, or nonprofit says, "We need to raise $XX million to buy or build this or that and no one has talked to the donors." The problem surfaces when no one has considered asking the top donors what they think, nor has anyone researched to see if the goal is feasible, desirable, or attainable. Instead, they sit in a room and say, "I think that $80 million would be great; let's launch a capital campaign and raise the money." They have no idea whether 30% or even 60% of their donor base believes in the cause in which they are asking them to give their hard-earned philanthropic money.

In Larry's situation, there was no success for such a campaign launched in this fashion. His campaign failed and Larry, admirably, stayed on the job. In time, Larry encouraged his supervisors and board to pay for a professional third-party feasibility study, employing a campaign case statement and related case for support documentation to determine if the university could raise $20 million instead of $80 million and for a more focused outcome-based missional need. In performing the feasibility study with forty-five households, Larry had donors who expressed changes to the campaign and eventually made large pledge commitments. The donors informed the university that they didn't support buying the property across the street, but a new building, and a new athletic field made perfect sense as it related to enrollment and graduate outcomes. Eventually, they launched the redesigned capital campaign, and they came out of the initial fundraising phase and had raised $12 million. Then they announced the public phase of the campaign to raise the necessary $8 million. Four years down the road, they were successful with a completed $20 million capital campaign.

Fundraising has a short game and a long game. Committing to a donor-centric philosophy means you must understand, respect, and involve your most loyal and connected donors. If you refuse to include your donors in the decision making and allow them to see themselves as partners, you are playing the short game. Donors today don't want to play a transactional philanthropic game. It is not the 1950s featuring the Rockefellers and Carnegies. Philanthropy was new then and people wanted to be a part of it no matter how it was organized. However, today's donor wants to be a part of the process, understand the impact, and enjoy the outcome. They want to participate as what I have termed "venture philanthropists, entrepreneur philanthropists, or grunge philanthropists." Today's donors want to be heard, listened to, and they want to be in the mix as a valued and involved partner. They do not want to be simply "voluntold." In a later chapter, I will define and describe in detail the "venture, entrepreneur, and grunge philanthropist."

Today's donor-centric partnership is true for capital campaigns, annual funds, and appeal letters. If you are not intentionally donor-centric, then you are not going to be successful. There is a right way to do this, and yes, it takes a little bit of effort. It may take longer, and you will have to be patient, but the outcome is vastly better than the immediate and will be sustainable for the future.

Dr. John Jackson was my president at William Jessup University when I transitioned from William Jessup to Colorado Christian University. During our last one-on-one session, John verbally blessed me. It was John who took a chance in hiring me as vice president for WJU. To this day, John periodically contacts me to encourage me. During that final one-on-one session Dr. Jackson told me "Eric, when I hired you, I never thought that it would be your radio background that would make you a successful Fundraiser."

"John, what do you mean by that?" I asked

"I am referring to your ability to be intuitive, logistical, strategic, and to do the blocking and tackling that it takes to be successful over time. I knew when I hired you that people would know you from your tenured media career and I knew you could raise money because you did that politically for a number of years. I knew people would trust you because you lived on the air in a fishbowl life for fifteen-plus years. But I never knew you could construct the fundraising logistics, processes, and systems like you have. Where did that come from?"

I wasn't expecting such glowing comment from him, "Every single day on talk radio I used something called an hourly format clock. The clock was a visual reminder that my job was to be audience-focused, build the number of listeners each hour, and increase (or retain) each listeners' time spent listening to my radio station. Each hour would build upon itself in content, conversation, and efforts to reach remedies and solutions for our country."

John asked, "Eric, how does this convey to what you have done at WJU?"

I elaborated, "For nearly 22 years of talk radio – every day, every week – I would program my performance toward the audience by employing audience-centric strategies in every segment of every hour. I was intentionally building listenership (and listening), building input, building callers, building a topic and an ultimate solution. My most important job was to get listeners to retain each hour, each day, each month, and each year. I went as far as to build systems to stay connected with my listeners after the show was over and during the weekends. I offered focus groups, or community building events, to help listeners meet listeners and to hear from them personally.

In the final segment of each Friday's program, I would pull listeners onto the show and ask them to walk through a current topic. As they went through this process, they could identify and relate to it and tell thousands of listeners what they believed needed to be done. The entire talk radio format process was built to grow a radio audience, connect with them, offer them valuable content, and spend time with them on the air and off the air, getting to know their passions and ideologies. In the end, my radio listeners could feel the issues discussed, and they developed a personal, passionate desire to participate in each issue's resolution."

My talk radio experience tutored me on how to be a donor-centric Fundraiser. I learned that authenticity matters. Relationships matter. Outcome and impact matter and gathering other likeminded people matter. The goal was to bring people in, gather similar interests and ideologies, and instill in each of them a partnership in making the world a better place for others and for themselves. This is the same template that I employ at Colorado Christian University. It's a constant commitment of being donor-centric. A process that inverts the old school, myopic philanthropic traditions of years gone by. It's a process where you gather generous donors to partner with your nonprofit's mission by relating to them *from the winning side of the ask.*

A Critical Question

Why this book? I might be a bit Pollyanna-ish with my entrusted donor-centric philosophy and structural premise, but I truly believe it works if Fundraisers focus on the donor's joy of philanthropy. A multimillion-dollar donor herself, Lisa Greer agrees with me: "Wouldn't it be great to get to a place where organizations trust donors enough to be transparent, and donors trust organizations enough to let them lead?"[1] This ground is where Fundraisers and philanthropists realize that they really want the same thing. Both the organization and the donor want measurable outcomes, significant impact, and financial sustainability.

As you've read the stories in this introduction, have you recognized your own fundraising frustrations and repetitive errors? I ask this critical question because my intention in writing these pages is to stir you to action and move you to make changes in what you are doing. Then your nonprofit or mission or church or organization will gain the blessing of long-term relationships with your donors who

---

[1] Lisa Greer, *Philanthropy Revolution* (London: Harper Collins, 2020), 48.

become your investment partners. Let's turn the page and keep going in this process.

Chapter One

Two Different Lenses, Two Different Results

"We must first become agents of philanthropy itself by recognizing the need to nourish it over time – not just extract as much as we can, as soon as we can, while offering as little in return as we can get away with."[2] – Jim M. Langley, *The Future of Fundraising*

There are two primary ideologies to achieve success in fundraising.

As you read, the true stories presented in the introduction point to one ideology which I call the "short-sighted" populous lens.

When you enter the vocation of philanthropy, a new Fundraiser reads and grabs on to every piece of philosophy, process, and collection of trade secrets and best practices they can incorporate from books, webinars and live seminar events. They want to learn whatever they can to succeed at their new job. This mixture of "welcome to the field of Fundraising" always focuses on the goals of the nonprofit organization (NPO) or the success of the Fundraiser.

---

[2] Jim Langley, *The Future of Fundraising* (Denver, Colorado: Academic Impressions Publishers, 2020), 5.

The negative examples in the introduction are lived through the short-sighted lens. When you use this lens, you are immersed in a frenetic energy of Fundraising practices with a desperate attempt to accomplish some immediate success – to prove yourself to your NPO. By incorporating the short-sighted lens, you will raise some money, but you will be constantly focused on the NPO's immediate needs. You will not be building a process, or a department, that is sustainable for the future of your donor's philanthropic intentions.

There is great truth in the old saying, "desperate people do desperate things." I get it, I've been there. The outcome typically is a "reactive Fundraiser," one who is under tremendous pressure and stress with a demand for immediate results. The newly employed Fundraiser becomes self-focused and begins to operate like a salesman employing guilt-ridden leveraging that ultimately leads to a fundraising style characterized by ambushing perspective donors. Ultimately, it creates off-the-charts donor apathy.

Anyone can ring a bell outside with a red kettle and ask for a donation but operating as a skilled fundraising professional who is focused on sustainability versus immediate success is a learned practice; a practice of time-invested intentionality and not a single act of an emotional plea or pressured request(s).

Conversely, the sustainable, opposing lens is constantly farsighted. This person works strategically, with patience, confidence, and in sincere cultivation practices with a goal of becoming **a trusted donor advisor** over time. This type of Fundraiser sees each donor as an opportunity to cultivate the "win-win." She settles herself, builds integral relationships with each donor, and understands that the lor game, the far-sighted advisement, and the goal of building trust, clarity, and sincerity is what donors desire from each NPO representative.

In these pages, I have one goal – to teach you to be a **donor-centric Fundraiser!** I will provide various templates to raise your gaze from the temptation(s) of operating with a near-sightedness so that you can look through the far-sighted lens that sees everything in practices of longevity, sustainability, outcomes, and philanthropic impacts.

A Tale of Two Fundraisers

As we dive in, give me some room to create a composite of real life stories with two fictitious names, all to help make a point.

In the introduction, I focused on fundraising scenarios and fundraiser philosophies that describe the operations of a Fundraiser called **Michaela Myopias**. Myopias, whether she knows it or not, is destined to be a fundraising short-timer – a staffer who is self-centered and only looking for immediate results.

In contrast, the second fictitious name is someone called **Douglas Donerpherst.** This Fundraiser takes a completely different approach m Myopias, and employs a practiced focus which involves ing, building trust, and pursuing a long-term goal for greater ıd impact for both the NPO and the donor(s). For the far- ındraiser, each of his practices are built on relationships become transactional. Donerpherst becomes a trusted and is actively talking with various donors in the portfolio about what they want to do with their philanthropic passions.

In contrast, Myopias, the short-sighted Fundraiser, believes she can reach out to her donors and tell them a particular need for her organization and get a $10,000 check with a salesman-like approach. The farsighted Fundraiser, Donerpherst, instead walks into the first meeting and listens to his donor. During this session, he may not ask for anything, but instead focuses on understanding the donor's passions, desired outcomes, and ultimate impacts. His intention with the first meeting is not to collect a check but to learn, discover, build trust and hopefully come away with a second meeting. In between the first and second meeting, Donerpherst can consider the various needs within his organization and whether they fit the donors' intentions for his donations. Donerpherst considers if the NPO's needs are in alignment with the passions of the donor.

What Myopias doesn't understand is that each donor has a mission statement – just like the NPO she is representing. The donor wants to validate that you are a trusted donor advisor and if your NPO's mission is in alignment with their philanthropic mission. If the donor does make a gift they will want to see if you will follow their passion and desires as to what will be done with that first donation. Inside, the donor is asking, "Will my gift be appreciated, used correctly within the organization and will this Fundraiser follow my prescribed and described intention?"

Employing a quick ask, as Myopias often considers, may be the first and last donation she receives from this donor. Donerpherst understands that the initial test is not a donor's gift, but the performance and intentionality of the Fundraiser. Donerpherst understands human hearts are full of God-placed motivations and personal passions. It's the Fundraiser's responsibility to discover them through a professional relationship, sound research, asking good questions and listening to the donor's answers in order to understand the donor's desires.

After I've met with a donor three or four times, I have a better understanding of their passions and philanthropic desires. After a while, they are asking me to connect their gifts to my organization because I seem to understand them and what they want to do – and they are willing to begin to trust me.

This type of Fundraiser philosophy and relationship is called "**donor-centric fundraising**." In fact, when Fundraisers cultivate donor relationships in this way, many times the donor will egg the Fundraiser on and ask, "Mr. Donerpherst, do you believe your organization can actually solve the problems you state in your mission?" They ask such questions because in their mind the Fundraiser has transformed into a professional relationship as a trusted advisor. The donors will genuinely want a donor-centric Fundraiser's input about their philanthropic giving. I will tell a new Fundraiser over and over, that at this point in the cultivation process, the roles have switched. The ask will soon be coming from the other side of the table. The donor is offering all of the questions and seeking the answers.

The Fundraiser who uses this lens has switched from "getting gifts" *from* the donor to a "shared partnership" *with* the donor. The mindset is completely different when you use a donor-centric lens. I never take a donor to lunch hoping they will give me a check. Instead, I go to lunch hoping to build my relationship with the donor.

The keys between me and the donors (notice I did not say "my donors"), are relational, impactful, and measurable outcomes, instead of being focused on a single gift or check amount.

Another characteristic of a far-sighted Fundraiser is recognizing donor loyalty and highlighting it. Occasionally at lunch with a donor, I will bring a printout history of the various gifts to my nonprofit organization. I will highlight the total amount, and then personally, sincerely, and intentionally thank them as I report how the funds have been used to further their passion and desires. And again, I will express my gratitude for the loyalty in this relationship.

Later in the book, I will detail the various types of donor personalities. As I interact with a donor, I want to discover if he/she is a **traditional** philanthropist, a **venture** philanthropist, an **entrepreneur** philanthropist, or a **"grunge"** philanthropist. These four types are discovered by having a firm grasp on their social-economic status, age, demographics, or geography. Each type of donor requires a unique relationship. Knowing each donor's philanthropic personality is vital, especially if you want to be a far-sighted Fundraiser.

The far-sighted Fundraiser is not hurried or pressured. An hour and a half lunch of asking questions and listening is tremendously successful—and rewarding! It's all about understanding and sustaining the relationship. These types of Fundraisers create systems which remove stress (theirs and their donors), and instead instill opportunity and optimism. Sessions with donors are relaxed because there is no ambush or leveraged pressure to take immediate action.

When Douglas Donerpherst meets with a donor, he is constantly telling stories about the impact of gifts on the nonprofit or ministry or charity. He is always talking about the "giving experience" with donors who have long-term relationships with the organization. Through the relationships, he's laser-focused to gather personal information about his donor's birthday, wedding anniversary, comments about his new grandchild or the success of his children – even comments about past philanthropic experiences, and good or bad, outcomes.

These benchmark comments are flares for the Fundraiser on the importance the donor places on his or her philanthropic experiences. They should be an important portion of the "contact report" for future donor appointments the far-sighted Fundraiser desires.

A strategy and process are used to gather this detailed information about a donor for their confidential portfolio. Later in this book I will give the specifics about how to gather this information in what is called a "contact report," so the information is in a manageable format and useable for sustainable fundraising opportunities.

The Necessary Conversation

In the introduction, I talked about Henry, the CEO of the nonprofit who came to Stephen and told him to raise "x amount of money." Yet Stephen knew with the donors in his portfolio that he could only raise "y."

The hardest leadership trait for Fundraisers is the necessity to speak truth to power. Every Fundraiser needs the ability to communicate, clarify, and educate their supervisor. You need to help them understand that fundraising is a marathon-type of work and not a sprint. When your boss comes to you and asks you to "hit up the donors" for a gift, you may win the sprint (and raise some funds) but you will never win the marathon (and become donor-centric). What you *will be* successful at is creating donor apathy. Donor apathy surfaces when donors believe they are nothing more than an NPO's ATM card and the Fundraiser does nothing but asks for money without any understanding of the donor's expressed intentions, desired outcomes, and endgame impacts.

I will be the first to admit, it is not easy to speak truth to power, or to tell your boss that his request to raise a certain amount of money is impossible.

But it must be done.

For example, the Fundraiser sometimes needs to report to his supervisor, "I've studied my donor portfolio. We cannot raise $7 million. I believe we are better situated to raise $4 million, a much more realistic goal for us this fiscal year."

As a Fundraiser, you have to help your boss understand that instead of being short-sighted in your relationships, some changes instead need to be made operationally to the budget. "Because we are not going to receive $7 million from our donor base this year."

These conversations are admittedly not easy, but they are essential for effective long-term Fundraisers.

Many Fundraisers will face sleepless nights in this process before they have the gravitas to give their CEO this type of reality check. Instead of "ringing up donors" for the immediate real or perceived needs, you help them see that you are looking at the long-term sustainability and a different manner of philanthropic operation. As the lead Fundraiser you must get to this level of clarity and mutual trust with your boss – the NPO's CEO.

Later in this book I will focus on how to lead the fundraising team and how to manage each of them – which includes leading yourself first. Leading the team and leading yourself are vitally important. The hard conversations with your CEO or your fundraising team will be hard to schedule. But in the end, these conversations of candor produce better budgets, better collegial relationships, and much better donor-centric results for the organization.

In a small shop with you and two other Fundraisers or admin staff, let's say you have 2,500 active donors in the database. You will need to be clear with your supervisor and explain, "We can certainly push these donors to give and some of them will respond. Essentially with an urgent push, we will burn through their patience and drive them into an attitude every Fundraiser will encounter called *donor apathy*. It's where you may receive an immediate, smaller donation that ultimately erodes the donor's experience and trust, which ultimately reduces donor retention. Or we can take our time, build up trust through a donor advising relationship, and make sure we are donor-centric. It's a process, and one that does not happen overnight."

I encourage you to have this honest conversation with your CEO/President utilizing logical points that may resemble something like:

"I want to be transparent and trustworthy to our donors. I need the time to discover their philanthropic passions and how it matches our mission so they will be our partners in a long-term sustainable program of philanthropy. To build such a relationship takes time. We want our donors to be so enthusiastic about their partnership with us that they invite others to join them in this effort."

Having this type of candor and professional transparency with your supervisor is vital. It will be worth the stressful lead-up, the uncertain outcome, and the occasional reminder, but in the long run, you will be better positioned with your donors, as well as your supervisor.

Serving Donor Philanthropic Diversification

Through my work at Colorado Christian University, one of my donors, Norm, has varied philanthropic interests including the homeless, Christ-centered education, and providing clean water in third world countries. We've met on numerous occasions. During these appointments Norm mentioned that he wanted to give an end of the year gift to CCU. I followed up and said, "Norm, you also have an interest in the homeless and clean water. Is there some way I can help you satisfy those interests as well, as we head toward the close of the year?"

"How would you do that?" he asked.

"Have you met Micah, the new director of this ministry which works with the homeless in Denver? He's not connected to the University, but he's a great guy with an important mission."

"No, I haven't met him."

"Then let me see if I can schedule a lunch with you and Micah. I'll call you with some times, and we'll get that done."

I followed up and put that meeting together. After the meeting, Norm made a gift to this homeless organization.

A few days later, Norm called me and said, "I want to increase my gift to CCU because I'm so appreciative you put me together with Micah."

"Thank you, Norm. I also know someone who provides clean water in underdeveloped countries." Through email I connected Norm and a clean water ministry.

There was a reason for my distinct behavior in helping Norm make donations to two other NPO missions. My goal is to represent Norm's philanthropic intent and desired outcomes, not just my NPO's efforts – or my personal fundraising goals. In representing Norm's desires, I was performing through a far-sighted lens. I was intentionally focused on the needs and passions of the donor. As a donor-centric Fundraiser, I want to help my donors in any way I can—even if the gift goes to a different ministry. Why? Because that is how I rise to the level of becoming Norm's donor advisor and not simply a tradesman Fundraiser for my specific NPO.

Since our original conversation, Norm has called me numerous times and even mentioned a fourth ministry interest. I am more than pleased to help him. Later in the book I will help you understand a donor's priorities for their philanthropic giving. You can gain this insight through asking donors about their priorities in giving, while at the same time, asking about their desired outcomes, impacts, and additional priorities for their philanthropy. I will give a few of the specifics and proven systems for this information, and how it can be used with your donors. Even if your organization is the donor's number two or three priority, you can still earn a donor's trust by helping them with their other giving priorities. This is a vital part of being a far-sighted, relational, donor-centric Fundraiser -- and trusted donor advisor – the most prized goal in being successful in your profession.

As an example of this process, let me use the skills of actor Edmund Gwenn who played Kris Kringle in the Christmas classic *Miracle on 34th Street*. Gwenn's character, as Santa Clause in this classic movie, displayed some peculiar behaviors when he served as Macy's holiday St Nick attraction.

In the movie, Gwenn's character would refer Macy shoppers, guests, and children, visiting his Santa Claus store holiday house, to consider other New York department stores to purchase toys that Macy's did not carry or have in stock. As the movie depicts, Gwenn's "Santa behavior" increased sales for Macy's and it also gave the customers an increased trust and confidence in the brand of Macy's department store. Trust for Macy's grew to such a level that other department stores had to reciprocate and do the same type of referrals.

I know, I know, this situation is a storyline in a fictitious movie, but it perfectly illustrates what sincere donor-centric Fundraisers need to do for their donors and their donor's individualized philanthropic passions.

If we believe people are given wealth for the good of mankind and the glory of God's name, it should be spread around and not hoarded or collected. Moses reminds us of this reality in Deuteronomy 8:18, "But remember the Lord your God, for it is he who gives you the ability to produce wealth." As a donor advisor, it's my job to think about the donor as much as I do my nonprofit organization. If the donor knows I have their best interest and trust in this process, then they will turn to me repeatedly for my advice to help them make decisions and deliver their generous donations and gifts. They will trust me with their decisions surrounding the utilization, impact, and outcomes of their wealth.

Terri had once given an $18,000 gift to CCU for veteran students. She wanted to make another gift and asked my advice. "There are a couple of churches that I want to make certain have enough funds during the pandemic. Do you know the pastors of these churches?" Then she named three different congregations.

"I don't know those pastors, but I'll find out and get back to you." I found the information and gave it to Terri. She contacted those pastors and made her donations. Later, she called me and affirmed she still wanted to give the $18,000 donation to veterans at CCU, *and* she wanted to make this gift *every year*. Ultimately, she was thanking me for getting the names of pastors so she could give to those churches. And I was thanking Terri for her generosity to families of veteran

CCU students. The relationship entered a new level of trust, respect, and philanthropic longevity. The far-sightedness provided a platform for synergy to develop between the donor and the Fundraiser.

The Importance of Job Titles

I believe being far-sighted and donor-centric includes our job titles. If you're building a philanthropic team, one of the most important things you need to consider is your job titles.

For many years, I followed the rule of thumb within fundraising titles such as Major Gift Officer. I would call a donor and begin, "Hi, this is Eric Hogue, Senior Director for Major Gifts for Colorado Christian University."

It turned out to be an immediate barrier to overcome.

The problem with using 'major gift officer' is that the donor(s) didn't see their name -- or their passion -- in my job title. The unspoken information which comes through with that type of job title is that any ensuing invitation for a time to get together over lunch, the donor immediately expects that he or she will be asked to make "a major gift."

I'm convinced bad, uncreative, job titles are very short sighted and hurt a Fundraiser's cultivation process. Later in this book I will explain how the CCU University Advancement team has changed a majority of our team's titles. With a slight adjustment, donors suddenly see an NPO representative who can help them with their philanthropy and not expect a transaction of giving. Through donor-centric job titles, donors understand I am not only interested in helping them with my particular nonprofit, but the Fundraiser's role is much broader than just the niche of collecting donations. Updated, donor-centric job titles help donors understand the professional aspect of the philanthropic relationship, whether it includes my organization or not.

Constantly Gather Information

The far-sighted Fundraiser is constantly working to gather additional information about their donors. This type of Fundraiser wants to foster relationships instead of being a soft- or hard-core salesman.

Mark Dillon wrote in *Giving and Getting in the Kingdom of God*, "Getting is not talking someone out of money that they don't want to give."[3] When your cultivation practice is grounded in donor-centric values this lens separates the salesperson from the donor advisor and it creates a trusted confidante for your prized donors.

Again, let me quote Mark Dillon. There are "those who *live off philanthropy,* versus those who *lived for philanthropy.*"[4] Near-sighted Fundraisers *live off philanthropy.* Far-sighted Fundraisers *live for philanthropy.* In my opinion there is only good philanthropy or bad philanthropy. There is no middle ground. Later in this book we will discuss the attitude of the Fundraiser and how her motivations play into good or bad outcomes.

Become A Better Listener

---

[3] Mark Dillon, *Giving and Getting in the Kingdom of God* (Chicago, Illinois: Moody Press, 2012), 41.
[4] Dillon, *Giving and Getting in the Kingdom of God*, 37.

We have two ears and one mouth. As an extrovert, I love a great conversation, but I have constantly trained myself to listen and ask probing questions when I meet with a donor. My curiosity about this donor is critical. Each donor meeting should produce a list of new or deeper understandings of that person. Each of us need to become a better listener, and this characteristic comes through continued practice.

After I finish meeting with a donor, I spend an additional thirty minutes to capture detailed information into a "contact report," which as I mentioned, I will detail in a later chapter. These notes capture what I heard, what I learned, what I noticed in non-verbal expressions, what I should remember, and actions I should consider for future donor engagement and discovery sessions.

Instead of the often-promoted two-minute elevator speech about your organization, it's much better for that donor to come away from your meeting knowing their passions have been heard and you, as a trusted partner, are going to help them with their philanthropy. On occasion I will send the donor a thank you letter and touch upon the items I heard, learned, and determined to be in representation of our conversation together. This type of post-meeting communication is another way to show the donor your commitment to their passionate philanthropy.

Earn Trust with Honesty and Transparency

As a Fundraiser, you must earn trust through honest and transparent conversation. The typical donor is suspicious of your fundraising motives. Your appropriate, caring, and big-picture actions prove your motives.

The Winning Side of "the Ask"

The beginning of long-term trust starts right here!

Every college and university operates annual fund campaigns. Gifts to this type of fund are usually unrestricted and ultimately go to the university's day-to-day, fundraising administrative, or operational budget. Many universities label this fund as a "scholarship fund." To be clear, it can benefit student scholarships, but in most cases, it does not.

Early in my career in higher education fundraising, one of my donors, Robert, was bemoaning how students were graduating with large amounts of debt and bondage when they entered the workplace. He asked, "If I give to the university scholarship fund, is all of that money going to go toward student debt?"

As an *in*experienced Fundraiser, I said, "It goes to a fund that supplements freshmen coming into the university every year."

Leaning back in his chair, Robert said, "That is not what I asked. If I give you a $5,000 check, will those funds go directly to pay a student's tuition?"

Back then, I was near-sighted and wanted to get this $5,000 gift for the university fund (and the assumed win). We had a projected need of a million dollars of operational funds which would be used for a wide variety of applications. I went back and forth attempting to find a way to get Robert's gift. He was looking for an honest answer and ended up not making any gift at all. I was focused on getting the gift versus being far-sighted and honestly addressing how the campaign worked as an unrestricted annual fund that supplemented the university's institutional financial aid – better known as a university's *discounted tuition rate*. The student receives the soft-money tuition "discount," and the university receives the actual dollars in donations to be added to the operational budget as unrestricted philanthropic income. This process is not unethical, it is just (a bit) insincere for the lead Fundraiser to represent accurately and transparently. Since this early career episode, I have adjusted the construct, brand, and communication(s) involving unrestricted annual funds.

Through this hard-earned experience, I learned the importance of being completely (and painfully) transparent and honest with every donor. I could have directed Robert toward an endowed scholarship which goes directly to a student, but my early years were -- again -- focused on the immediate and the NPO's needs, not the donor's desires.

Today's donors are savvy. They listen carefully to your answers to their questions. They simply want the truth.

Think about people in your life where you have a high level of trust; how quickly you can get to deep levels of conversation. As a Fundraiser, you must give donors this type of "trusted relationship," even if it costs you the gift. If there is a better nonprofit which is more of a match for that donor's passion, then suggest the other organization. Again, this type of earned trust will give you position for future gifts because you are building a professional donor advising relationship on truthfulness and trustworthiness.

If your organization is in debt, tell the truthful story to the donor. For example, say you know they are interested in student-athletes, and you also know the soccer team is always underfunded. You suggest, "You could help our soccer program with a $10,000 gift each year to help their travel budget; it would help them cut their operational costs."

If they counter with, "I don't like to give to debt." Then you respond, "It sounds like this program isn't right for you. That is, if you want to give to programs which are growing, this is not your best option. Your gift would be better utilized being associated with our science program and its enrollment increases and high demand nationally."

It is only through a forthright conversation will you have such an honest donor dialogue.

In contrast I've had countless conversations where I will say, "That program (campaign) never breaks even."

In this situation, the donor responds, "That's where I want to give my gift because I want to see that program break even and even prosper."

If you know your donors well enough, some of them will give to underfunded programs where others will not. The only way you will know this information is from building a relationship and not making a short-sighted request.

Store the Details of Every Donor Meeting

This point is so important, I'm going to mention it now for the third time in this chapter: After a meeting with a donor, every Fundraiser should complete a contact report about their meeting.

For anyone who knows me, they know I'm a bit "countercultural." Traditionally, these reports are pithy and to the point. My reports are lengthy and detailed in our database. They're better understood as a lengthy journaling for our team's customer relations management system (CRM). These reports should feature a donor's interest, experiences, emotions, and desired outcomes. Each of my reports are written as though it was the final report in this donor's file. If another Fundraiser becomes the contact for Mr. and Mrs. Jones, the new Fundraiser can read my previous contact reports and quickly – accurately – learn intimate details about them.

Conventional wisdom may say, "No one reads them" or "I don't have the time." If you don't have the time, then your donor portfolio is too large, and you are working with too many people. These contact reports are building a diary of the relationship between you and your donors. I have several donors who are in a second marriage because their first wives died, or they divorced. I know what their first gift to CCU was designated toward, what they did for a living, whether they're retired, how many children and grandchildren they have.

These details are important to the maturation of the donor relationship and need to be captured in the contact report. The carefully crafted donor report is the "secret sauce" for each Fundraiser. From my experience, ninety percent of donor advisors don't invest this time in drafting a legitimate contact report.

I believe in a completely different strategy and process in crafting a utilitarian contact report than other Fundraiser colleagues. My contact reports are intentionally colorful, very detailed, often very lengthy and will sometimes describe the emotional aspects in our meetings. I carry 75 to 100 donors in my portfolio, and my reports read more like a diary versus a static and sterile report. I believe short, pithy, one paragraph contact reports to be, well, lazy. You are underserving your NPO, and it is evidence that the encounters and the relationships are bothersome versus optimistically enjoyable. If you are bored as a Fundraiser, you need to look for another vocation, or line of work.

I reviewed a recent contact report with Don, one of our lead donors. He talked about his son and how his son is very busy and doesn't have much time for him. It was basically a rant about his disappointment with his adult child and their distant relationship – it had no direct relationship to Don's past donations or his philanthropic intentions. After our lunch, I wrote all of this information into Don's confidential contact report.

Our campus routinely hosts guest lecturers. Recently, Dr. Greg Smalley, a vice president of Marriage and Family Formation at Focus on the Family and a parent of a CCU student was coming to campus. He was going to teach about parents dealing with mid-life children. I thought about Don's story, looked in my CRM's contact report file for him to confirm our past conversation. I invited Don to attend the lecture to hear Dr. Smalley's lecture and to be encouraged that our relationship was more than just donation dollars. It's this type of far-sighted donor advisor activities you need to incorporate as a donor-centric Fundraiser.

How I Prepare Before I Ask

The donor knows that, eventually, you will be asking them to donate to your organization. I like to inform the donor as soon as possible, or as appropriate, that I want to help them with their philanthropy. As I understand their passion and what they want to do with their giving, I begin to advise them. Additionally, I kindly inform each donor that *I will never ask them for a donation without preparing them first*. Usually, during the previous lunch or meeting, I will ask them if I can "make a proposal during our next meeting." If the donor consents to my asking, then I come to that next session with a detailed proposal of my request. In essence, I ask if I can make an ask of the donor. I will never catch a donor off-guard in respect to their generosity toward my organization by springing an unexpected ask or proposal on them without their knowing and approval to do so. This "ask if you can make an ask" concept is something that needs to be established early in your relationship; maybe the second or third meeting together.

What happens when I prepare the donor for my request? Each time, the donor has agreed to receive a donation request from me and is never surprised. During my career as a Fundraiser, I have employed this practice hundreds of times. I am happy to report that, in most cases, the donor comes prepared to either donate or make a pledge. When someone is shepherded properly, they are always willing to hear a proposal from a trusted donor advisor.

I've made this ask in a variety of different ways such as on the phone or in a text or via email. These donors give me permission to make the ask because they trust the relationship that we have developed over time. When I make this ask, sometimes they respond, "I can't do it all right now. Can I consider a gift spread out over the next three years?"

Even if the donor makes the gift over several years, it is still a very positive response to my ask. I'll take any pledge over three years because I get three more years of the relationship and three more years of reporting philanthropic outcomes about the impact their dollars are having. It gives me more time to tell student stories to the donor and about the overall success of my NPO.

Long-term donor-centric relationships work, both for the donor and the NPO!

Mastery Takes Time and Consistent Growth

Using the right lens is the first step in your journey toward successful Fundraising. The temptation is to act, or react, too fast, and with a not-as-good-as-it-should-be-motivated impulse. Sure, as the Fundraiser you have goals, projects, and projections you need to reach in donations. I am not denying the struggle of projections and performance. It's real and it's a constant reality. What I have learned is that this struggle is not an either/or, it's a both/and. Yes, you grow impatient and yes, you must teach yourself to wait, be patient and respectful – trusting the right lens and the right approach.

Recently, my high school football coach passed away. Paul Starkey was a coaching legend in northeast Ohio. He won numerous Federal League Championships as head coach at Louisville Senior High.

In 1981 Coach Starkey led our senior class to one of his many Federal League Championship seasons. We had some quality talent on the team, but not great talent. I remember Coach Starkey being interviewed by a local radio station about our team and our chances to defeat two larger schools featuring better overall talent on their team rosters.

To the reporter he gave the usual rote answers while being interviewed for the radio audience. After the reporter concluded his final question and Coach's prepared his answer, he turned off the recorder. The reporter asked, "Paul, do you really believe you can beat Hoover High and Perry High in back-to-back weeks?" Coach responded (after asking if it was off the record), "I do. We are a team of great overachievers and patient seniors – they have waited a long time for these two games and this opportunity." Coach Starkey then added, "You have to understand that I have been coaching against Coach Hertler (Hoover High) and Coach DeMaree (Perry High) for a number of years – I know them well. There will come a time in each game where we will have our guys in position to win the game."

He was right.

Louisville won both games with key plays late in the ballgame. Coach Starkey prepared his team, but he also prepared himself. He was patient, respectful of the other coaches, and knew when to call "the right play at the right time." He had a lens that was future-game-focused, not self-focused. He always trusted the process in the same way the characteristics I've highlighted in this chapter do. It takes personal development time, requires consistent growth, and has a firm commitment to a donor-centric process. If you stay focused and grow consistent in developing the far-sighted lens in Fundraising, you will be successful in the end.

In the next chapter, you will discover the deeper, philosophical, lessons about what it means to become sincerely donor-centric.

The Winning Side of "the Ask"

Chapter Two

Commit to a Donor-Centric Philosophy

"Our success is built on quality relationships. We communicate openly and truthfully in a timely manner. We encourage each other and have fun together. We are helpful and compassionate. We treat others the way we want to be treated." – Jeff Coors, *God is My CEO*

Fundraisers can often be infected with a virus of myopia. Normally, a Major Gift Officer earns a good salary and gains a sound position of leadership and organizational respect. Upon entering the world of philanthropy, she is immediately introduced to various gimmick strategies, and she can be lured into believing her skills and expertise is central to the success of fundraising. In many ways, novice Fundraisers fall into the same trap as Narcissus, the hunter from Greek mythology. If you're familiar with the story, this accomplished and handsome man had a wise mother who recognized his standout appearance and skillset. In fact, his mother proclaimed that Narcissus would live a long life if he never saw his own handsome image. Throughout his childhood, his mother often warned Narcissus of this simple yet important truth: never look at yourself in a mirror.

The Winning Side of "the Ask"

One day, Narcissus traveled deep into the forest. He was traveling into the woods to get away from being controlled by another's requests and interests. From his journey, he became physically exhausted and thirsty. Following closely behind Narcissus was an exiled seductress named Echo. When she saw Narcissus, she wanted to proclaim her love for him but couldn't speak because of a previous curse placed upon her. She was called Echo because this lovely woman's only means to make sound was to echo someone else. As Narcissus walked through the woods, she followed him. Narcissus eventually came to a calm stream and knelt to get a drink of water. As he leaned toward the stream, he saw his image reflected in the calm water. His reflection initiated the myopic curse. When he saw his image, he proclaimed, "I love you" to himself. As Echo heard Narcissus repeat over and over, "I love you. "Echo quickly responded, "I love you, too." But her words of affection were too late and had no effect on Narcissus. The young man was caught up in the curse of his own appearance and ability and never noticed the beautiful Echo sitting beside him.

During my career in fundraising, I've met a good number of Major Gift Officers (MGOs) who turned into narcissists. These myopic Fundraisers were focused on their own skills, specialized strategies, and their "*secret sauce*" personalities. These individuals loved to talk about their successes and pontificate on their great formulaic theories. While they probably won't use these exact words, as these Fundraisers interact with donors, their attitude is, "you are really fortunate to be working with me so I can help you with your giving." With these self-centric fundraising personalities, successful philanthropy is all about them, their skills, and their successes. With this attitude, these MGOs act like Narcissus – they constantly miss Echo's affectionate plea while they focus on themselves. These Fundraisers miss the passion, love, and pursuit of a donor who – in the end – cannot grab the MGOs' attention away from their admiring reflection of themselves. This happens when the Fundraiser believes that successful fundraising is all about them and their amazing (myopic) strategies. They believe they can talk anyone into giving a large gift because of their personality, their conversation and their myopic style.

Let me be clear: **successful fundraising rests with the passions of the donors and not the self-seeking personality of the Fundraiser.** As a Vice President with many well-intentioned MGOs on my team, I've had to transition a number of Fundraisers because they have gone down this narcissistic path. Additionally, over the past few years, I have attended numerous fundraising seminars and workshops. Some were worthy – but most were poorly planned and orchestrated. Frequently, these "conferences" feature fundraising consultants who are looking for future clients from the those who pay to attend these skill-growing events. I support the proposition of tenured Fundraisers mentoring new, younger, more inexperienced Fundraisers. In many ways, these types of events are legitimate – when orchestrated correctly, rightly, and positioned with content for the right reasons.

I must be transparent: not all philanthropic consultancies are the same. Each of these heavily marketed events exhibit different motives and strategic systems. I have found that a majority of these seminars and workshops do nothing more than build the egos and humanistic confidences of the Fundraiser. They ignore, entirely, the vital role of the donor and his/her, philanthropic passion, desired outcomes, and their prescribed intentional impact.

The Fundraiser-Centric Cycle

Within many fundraising circles, they teach a process called a "Fundraiser-centric cycle" which is completely dependent upon the skill set and ability of the Fundraiser. In fact, there is nothing in this cycle that is donor-centric. Instead, the Fundraiser-centric cycle process targets the donor and convinces (persuades) the donor to give to you to meet your NPO's expressed needs and desires.

Typically, when attending these seminars and reading the conference materials, the Fundraiser-centric cycle features a four-step process for successful donor cultivation process. It is exampled here in this diagram.

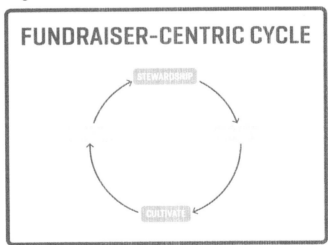

Identification: In this initial step, the Fundraiser's aim is to discover the level of wealth capacity of the donor. The implied method is for the Fundraiser to determine how quickly he or she can access a major gift for the needs of the NPO. The initial step is gift-focused versus donor-focused. The Major Gift Officer usually asks himself, "What kind of donation can I ask for and what size of gift can I receive?" The immediate substance of the relationship is transactional and not relational. If you employ this cycle for your fundraising practices, you are looking for the reward, the big donation, and the pride that comes if you land a large donation. It is immediately about the Fundraiser and their skills. It builds pride, ego, and self-focus – and experienced donors can recognize these bothersome traits right away. At the close of this chapter, I will discuss inappropriate pride versus appropriate pride as a successful donor-centric Fundraiser.

Cultivation: The second step in this cycle screams Fundraiser immediacy, "How fast can I ask my donor to give a large donation?" Many Fundraisers use the term "cultivation." This term strikes me as peculiar, mainly for the fact that the word means "the culmination of a process." Why is this the second step goal for the Fundraiser? In this cycle, Fundraisers are taught "cultivation" is a single, or short, action *in time* and not an investment *over time*. Cultivation becomes the goal, versus discovery and building trust over a lengthy period of time.

Solicitation: The third term in the standard Fundraiser-centric cycle is solicitation. To me, it is one of the most offensive words in the process and it screams of a sales approach to raising funds. Webster's dictionary describes solicitation as, "To make petition; to approach with a request or plea, to strongly urge, to entice or lure, or to proposition." Do we really desire our MGOs to make pleas, strongly urge, or "lure in" making a proposal to a well-intended donor? This word positions the Fundraiser as a transitional salesperson who is going to "close the deal" by making a "strong, bold ask." Is the Fundraiser (MGO) going to guilt the donor into giving? Is the Major Gift Officer (MGO) encouraged to make the donor feel uncomfortable until they give to the nonprofit or ministry? I am sorry to report that, in a few circles, this is actually the technique taught and the desired outcome. Solicitation is simply a sales tactic for a gift and not legitimate philanthropy. This portion of the cycle is focused on the one-time gift and isn't about a long-term relationship.

Stewardship: In most conference coursework, Fundraisers are trained to express their appreciation to the donor for their gift in an official gift receipt letter for the donor's tax purposes. If the gift is large enough, the donor also receives a personal letter from the director or CEO and/or president of the nonprofit organization. This expression of gratitude is the final action of the process. In this cycle, the teaching is for the Major Gift Officer to "steward the gift" forward, but this is the wrong expression and, again, the wrong focus. Stewardship is not about the gift, it's about understanding the passions and interests of the donor. But if you never discover them, or identify them, you don't know how to steward them forward.

One of my former Major Gift Officers, Michael, had lunch with Mr. and Mrs. Smith and they gave him a $50,000 donation to the university. In my office, I met with Michael as he described his fourth lunch with Mr. and Mrs. Smith, "During the lunch, I made the ask and they gave me a check for $50,000."

"Congratulations, Michael," I said. "Great work but let me ask you . . . what's the gift for?" For an instant, Michael had a surprise expression on his face, then he quickly answered, "It's for the university. We can use it any way we want."

I pressed a bit more, "I find it peculiar because $50,000 is the largest gift Mr. and Mrs. Smith have ever given to the university. Did they give any direction about where they want us to use these funds?"

Despite my pressing the issue, Michael repeated, "No. They just said, you can use it at the university in any way you see fit."

"Michael, the gift strikes me as unusual. Do you mind if I give them a call?"

"No, go ahead," he said.

The next day, I called the Smiths. "On behalf of the University, I want to thank you for the $50,000 gift. This is your largest gift to us, and we are so grateful for your partnership. We were blown away by your generosity. Again, thank you so much. Allow me to ask, did you have any intention with that gift?"

There was a period of silence as they considered how to answer. "We really do have some ideas about how the funds are used but

Michael didn't ask us about it. We figured he had some pressing needs in mind and we left it at that"

"Well, let me ask. What do you want the $50,000 to do?"

They told me about a friend, Mary, who wanted to go to college and become a youth pastor but couldn't complete her degree.

"What is Mary doing now?" I asked.

"She's a barista at a Starbucks downtown. Occasionally we see her and go there to have some tea and coffee."

I returned to the use of the gift, "How do you want the university to use your $50,000?"

"We'd like those funds to go into student scholarship to help students who are in the School of Theology and desire to become youth pastors or go into world missions."

From my work in fundraising, I knew Michael had followed the Fundraiser-centric pattern of identification, cultivation, solicitation, and stewardship. He never asked the Smiths or listened to their intention for their gift. I'm certain Michael's outgoing personality dominated the conversation with this quiet, older couple. They just thought they'd give the $50,000 to the university because the Lord told them to do it. They trusted the Lord for how those funds were to be used. This situation happens over and over. The Fundraiser is focused on "getting the gift" but doesn't discover or appreciate the intentions of the donor, or their passion for giving.

Later I met with Michael and directed him to schedule another meeting with the Smiths, but this time with a different focus. I asked him to listen and learn how the Smiths wanted the University to use their gift. Listen to their stories, their hearts, and their passion – if you don't hear it, ask them! This somewhat embarrassing experience proved to be a valuable lesson for Michael, for the Smiths, and for me.

A Donor-centric Philosophy

Over my fourteen-plus years in philanthropy, I've designed a different Fundraiser cycle which is a five-stage donor-centric cycle. As the Fundraiser/MGO employs this process, he will discover an authentic and strictly professional relationship. This cycle is not self-focused on the Fundraiser but is intentionally focused on the donor. Let's define the five areas:

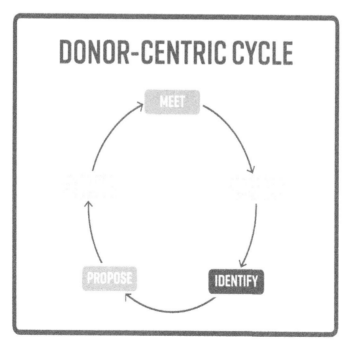

1. The Meet. If your goal is to become intentionally relational versus transactional, you need to make the first encounter a human event. It's not hard to be human; just be yourself as you interact with this other person.

You are not:

> ➢ Thinking about how much the donor is worth.

> ➢ Trying to determine "What's the angle with this person?"

> ➢ Using some self-contrived, self-centered fundraising tactic.

Instead, you are exploring and building a relationship through a free-flowing conversation at a physical face-to-face meeting. As you share stories, you can grow to like them, and they can like you. With every new person, there are many areas to explore and learn about. Often, I begin asking about their hometown. If they have never moved from this place, I want to hear why. Was this decision a positive one or are they like a reluctant George Bailey (from "It's a Wonderful Life"), "I always wanted to move, but duty called, and I had to stay put"?

As you meet this person and learn about them, you will gain much insight and information when someone talks about their childhood, upbringing, and the hometown they loved – or disliked. Also, you will learn about their politics, educational journey, parenting skills and experiences, as well as their career, vocation, and work journey. With each topic there is much to explore in the conversation. It is critical for you to listen and ask questions more than you speak with this person.

As an extrovert from a talk radio background who hates dead air or silence, it is easy for me to talk the entire time with a new donor—

yet that is not the purpose of this session. With intention, I ask questions and follow-up questions to engage the donor as I actively listen to them and their answers, comments, and opinions. Some donors will not ask about you because they are extreme introverts. You need to learn that this reality is a good result. I love working with introverted donors. They may never ask about me, but they do ask about the university. Usually, in 90% of the cases, the donor is going to ask questions about the Fundraiser, if the relationship is a sincere meeting. As you interact, be transparent and don't try to impress your guest or embellish your own story. Your donor-centric dialogue and conversational actions will show that you desire to be a professional acquaintance.

There is some preparation needed before the appointment; some diligent homework. Before your first meeting you will need to do some research on your guest. You will gather a basic understanding of who they are, what they do, and why they love to do it. From my radio background I have always appreciated the Larry King rule of research: Don't research too much, just enough to know who you are talking to and what topics are friendly and warm. I encourage you to leave some topics and areas of introduction unknown so you can ask questions and learn during your time together. You intentionally make the time together about stories, life experiences, brief personal and family bios, simple friendly questions, and honest reactions that lead toward a sincere understanding and appreciation of your guest.

The first time I met Mr. Jacob Hill, we spent two hours talking about his property development. He was building a new resident development where the homes were fitted with solar panels on the roof and a unique rainwater capture system. I sincerely wanted to know how the water was captured and how it was used and reused for the development. He told me about the design of a community cistern, or underground tank, that stores the water for later use by the neighbors for irrigation and property washing. I found the whole process extremely fascinating. With every subsequent meeting with Mr. Hill, I ask about the progress of his development and updates on the rainwater capture system.

Recently, Mr. Hill informed that his development installed colored lights on the street corners. The colors change if there is a neighborhood threat, break-in, or some other emergency situation. Everyone in the community knows what the colors mean and can take the appropriate action. What a marvelous idea – and again, what a great conversation to share over lunch.

Mr. Hill is a donor to the university, but his philanthropic passions toward CCU are in their infancy. He has been open about his investment into the development project and the upfront costs for him and his business partners. He has stated, "I don't have the means to be a big help to CCU at this time, but in time I hope I can be." We have a great donor relationship. It is professional, interesting, futuristically philanthropic, and always a deep dive when we share lunch.

This first step in the cycle, the meet, should always happen in person. Sometimes I meet donors over a meal while other times we speak informally for twenty minutes during an event. From my experience, you never meet someone via email. I'm writing this book during the tail end of the pandemic, so I understand that sometimes our only personal alternative is digital or utilizing video-conferencing like Zoom. But I'm a bit old school. It's hard to really meet someone if it is not in-person. The only way to develop a donor-centric relationship is talking with your donor face to face, handshake to handshake, and non-verbal to non-verbal.

The digital platform comes into play when you are determined to gather basic background information on your prized donors by using Google, Zillow, LinkedIn, news websites, press releases, and digital newspaper articles. You can also employ a wealth screening platform subscription that collects all public information surrounding your specific searches. When operating a prospect research and wealth screening, make sure to include relatives, family names, and former places of employment. Again, this is preliminary and for the purpose of gaining a brief reference before you meet your donor. The meeting is still the main source of discovery and understanding between you and the donor's life, passions, and philanthropic intentions.

2. Discovery. This second step in a donor-centric cycle can happen as early as the initial meeting. Remember, you are not meeting with this individual to become close friends. Friend making is NOT fundraising. This meeting is for the purposes of donor-centric philanthropy. The donor is aware of your purpose, and you should know it and act like it. During the initial meeting, I usually pull out my pen and a small stack of index cards. I will often ask, "Can I make a few notes? This is interesting to me." Some donors will ask me what I'm going to do with my notes. I explain how after our conversation I write a summary of what I learned for my records for future reference.

Other donors when they hear about these reports ask, "Can I see what you wrote?" Each time I tell them that I will go back to my office and type the notes into what I call a "Contact report," and will send it to them personally. In some cases, the donors begin to open up and share more and more content and details after I begin to take notes. The additional information is invaluable.

I tend to ask questions about their intentions, desired outcomes, and future impacts they want from their philanthropy. The discovery process involves very active listening. In my notes, I clarify statements and note any/all expressed life chronologies. I encourage MGOs to be authentic with reactions. If your emotions are moved, that is good, but don't fake emotions. Be authentic, real, honest – in a phrase, just be yourself!

Try to get your guest to a comfortable stage of talking about themselves, their businesses, family, dreams, and hopeful future. As I stated earlier, it is perfectly fine to ask a donor about their philanthropic intentions and pursuits, because you are not asking them for a gift or donations. Make certain to clarify your guests' statements by being inquisitive. Donors appreciate interest and integrity. Here's a little secret that I learned during my radio days: everyone loves to be interviewed without being told it is an interview. As you can see, it is enough to use your pen and one or two index cards. Through active listening with a notecard, I get my best contact reports.

Put Your Smart Phone Away

Almost everyone has a smart phone, but as I meet with donors, I take specific steps to lower the visibility of my phone. I do not use my phone to take notes, I use the notecards and a pen (old school). In fact, in sight of my guest I purposely turn off my ringer on my phone and put it face down on the table to my left, and somewhat out of reach. Because my phone is upside down, there is no temptation to look at it during my conversation and my guest notices my caging of my phone indicating to them (reminding me) this appointment is smart phone free. Your guest should see you are completely committed to your time together. If your phone is visible and it rings, or vibrates, your guest will see you ignore the call as you stay focused on them. People often ask about emergencies. Most smart phones have a feature where you can have your family's cell number(s) bypass the silent mode and ring aloud. You should utilize this setting permanently. If it rings with a family emergency, no donor will ever be upset by a family call getting through to you. I have had numerous donors comment in the affirmative after I have taken a call from my wife, daughters, or family member.

A Critical Emphasis

Throughout this entire process, no one has said anything about wealth or a gift or a donation (unless the donor broaches the topic). Instead, my focus is on actively listening, making physical or mental notes, and building a relationship with my guest. The meeting includes nothing intentional about a gift, donation, or campaign involvement. It's time America returns to meeting people for the purpose of getting to know them and appreciate them – business comes later, if at all.

3. Identify. During and after your meetings, take time to reflect on your donors' stories and the conversation content, which most should go into your contact report. During this stage, you begin to identify the donor's passions, personality, and character. Why is this person interested in your nonprofit organization and are they a fit or not to your NPO's mission and/or your fundraising campaigns? As you begin to identify their type, remember, it is not just about their wealth. The donor should fit your organization with their ideologies toward life and their intent to impact others for the good through your organization. I often review my previous encounter meeting notes (contact reports) and ask the donor in our second meeting to clarify their statements, or I use them to help the donor tell me more about themselves and their answers to my initial questions. This process reveals that you have thought about them during and after each meeting in this cultivation cycle.

One of my favorite topics is to ask my donor questions which allow me to emotionally experience their dreams and desires. For example, "I really want to learn more about your commitment to curing cancer. What is the source of this passion, where did it come from?" When you ask such a question, get ready because you are going to get a raw story and you will learn about an emotional event, or a commitment to a deceased loved one, or even a personal trauma in their life. They want cancer to stop or to bring about change or any number of other results from experiences in their life. These stories, experiences, and desires drive their philanthropy. In other opportunities, the donor may want to invest in an innovative method, or process, to rid the threat of cancer. They want to play the role of hero for others and rid the human race of the evil results of cancerous diseases.

Recently, I met a new donor couple in the later stages of their lives. During our third meeting, as we met for dinner, Betty expressed her father's recent passing and his service in World War II. Our previous discovery visits centered on the University's mission, academics, and its growing online platform for students nationwide to gain an undergraduate or graduate degree. Betty was intrigued with distant online learning, and that we have over 9,000 students nationwide in this school. Betty referenced her father over and over during my time at dinner with her and her husband. I knew she was considering a gift to support this vital adult learning platform.

"My dad was a business owner, and he would feel terrible about himself because he didn't attend college," she explained. "He would be doing business deals with CEOs who had graduated from Harvard, yet he had never got a degree. He felt intimidated because every other leader in the room had a degree or two. It never mattered to me. My dad was a war hero, and he didn't need a degree. To this day it drives me crazy that he felt this way and I don't want anyone else to feel that way."

I identified Betty's heartfelt passion for military and veteran students who were studying in our online program. During and after our third encounter, I returned to my office and asked for a few items of research on CCU's undergraduate and graduate military scholarship assistance programs. For our next meeting, I prepared a thank you card for our last time together and an expression of eager anticipation for our next luncheon. How do you think Betty responded? She was touched and immediately excited about the opportunity and the impact for future students. Today her father is honored, Betty's passion is fulfilled and active, and each year a growing number of CCU Online students are benefitting from her philanthropy.

4. Request to Propose. This is the next step in my donor-centric cycle. One of my primary fundraising rules in coaching a fundraising team is teaching each MGO how to prepare the donor for the proposal. I never ambush the donor; instead I prepare them ahead of time. Let's be honest: the donor understands what my job entails. They know that eventually I will make a proposal for a donation (aka: The Ask). Throughout each meeting and contact, I am intentional to keep the relationship professional. When the time is right, I gently say: "My role is to help you (the donor) fulfill your passion to do good with your generous philanthropy. My job is to understand what it is you want to do, and why."

In addition, I clearly communicate to each of them, "As we meet together, I promise I will never ask you for a donation without asking you about it ahead of time." Something like, "At our next meeting, if it is OK with you, I'd like to make a proposal. And if you affirm that it is OK to make one, I will come prepared to define, describe, and deliver a detailed proposal of my request."

With Betty, as we moved through the donor-centric cultivation cycle, the time was right for me to ask her about her military father and present a couple of offers or opportunities in line with her passions through CCU. A week ahead of our scheduled meeting, I contacted Betty and asked, "I have been thinking about your father. At CCU, we have 85 veterans currently enrolled in our CCU Online graduate school. In my research, I have discovered the number one reason for veteran students to withdraw before graduation. During our next meeting can I share my research with you and offer you a couple of ideas to help remedy this dilemma for veteran students at CCU?"

Every time I have asked a donor if I can make a proposal, they respond in the affirmative. They want to hear my proposed opportunity and they understand they have the right to say no to any or all of these options.

During our next luncheon, I offered Betty four options to support CCU Online students through our restricted scholarship campaign called the Hope Fund. I presented the proposals at lunch. As she read a few of the students' stories, Betty began to cry. Then she dropped her fork and quickly said, "Let's do this, Eric! I want to commit to $35,000 annually to be given equally to three married adult graduate students who are either veterans, or currently serving in our military."

I asked her, "Can we begin this before the end of this year?"

Reaching into her purse, Betty continued, "Yes, I actually came prepared with an initial check of $18,000 to give to you today. You said you were making an offer and I knew you knew my purpose for CCU and your military students." Through Betty's generosity to three students, they will receive scholarships helping to pay their tuition at the university.

5. <u>Engagement.</u> Reflecting back to the final stage of the traditional fundraising cycle is the term "stewardship," which I believe is both confusing and out of place because the donor sees this cycle as pure solicitation. I much prefer the word engagement, which is a term that conveys the continuing of the established relationship. I've seen many Major Gift Officers follow the donation after receiving the gift and they send a thank you letter without personally reaching out to the generous donor again. As the Fundraiser, I want to continue the relationship for the sake of the donor and for my NPO. My cultivation shifts into a grateful on-going engagement of gratitude, appreciation, and hopeful futures.

For every Fundraiser, you must address a few practical elements to express gratitude to your donor for their donation to (and through) your organization. Within 48 hours of the donation, it's standard operating procedure to send a personal, written, gift receipt letter (GRL) which also serves as an immediate receipt for the donor's purposes. In addition, you should make a personal phone call or send a handwritten thank you card or letter. For large donations, you should pull in your president, CEO, and/or director to the gratitude process. Your internal practices and processes need to create this step in expressing gratitude combined with a personal understanding of the donor's intentions.

A couple of weeks after their gift, you want to reach out to this donor again. Possibly your organization has a publication or a magazine or some other appropriate communication tool to forward to them in the meantime. When you mail this information, make sure you add a personal note such as "I thought these publications and pertinent information might encourage you in your giving through CCU." In this simple mailing, you are quickly establishing a process of 'reporting back' to the donor on impacts, outcomes, and possible future opportunities.

Sometimes I will invite a donor to a special event or webinar at the University which ties to their philanthropic interest(s). I ask, "What would you like to hear from the university?" In their contact report, I document their response. Each donor is different as to their preference. I have a few donors who don't desire to read their regular mail. They prefer to receive information via email, or some (usually younger demographics) a texted link. As you clarify these contact details, you are engaging them, and they know they are not forgotten but will be receiving ongoing communication. Your follow-up is not for another gift but clearly so they will be able to see the impact and on-going effort from their donation. This is engagement.

If you need a basic reminder to help you navigate your donor advisor role, you might consider a very simplistic "post donation check list of actions." Lynne Wester, from her book entitled *The Four Pillars of Donor Relations"* offers a few.[5] I have taken the liberty to embellish her work by labeling the post-gift actions as 1. Appropriate Acknowledgement, 2. Personal Impact Reporting, 3. Personal Recognition, and 4. Future Engagement. These four high-level steps of post-gift action take your donor advisory role into a deeper, more

---

[5] Lynne Wester, *Academic Impressions* (Denver, Colorado, 2019), 18.

trustworthy relationship with your donor. In the donor-centric world of philanthropy, there are no "simplistic, one-size-fits-all steps to success." There are only sincere relationships and intentional steps of gratitude after a generous donation is expressed to your organization.

Many Fundraisers are on the constant pursuit to actively locate new donors. Again, I remind you, the best donor is the one you have a donor-centric relationship with today. Once you engage them properly, they will stay with you (and your NPO's mission) for a good number of years. One of the key elements to maintain them post-donation is to sincerely engage and connect them to the impact and outcomes of their gift(s) for your NPO's mission. For example, ask them, "Would you like to volunteer? We have homecoming on campus. Our alumni department has created some welcome packets which need to be handed out to a parent dinner." Engaging them through volunteering, so they can experience your NPO's mission and the purpose of their giving, is a sound way of building toward the future and solidifying their role as donor and partner with your NPO.

I've had million-dollar donors tell me, "We'd love to meet the parents and the students. Count us in and we will do whatever needs to be done." They get no special treatment. They wear the same plastic name badge as everyone else on my team. They may work the buffet line or stuff "Week of Welcome" new student gifts for incoming freshman students and their parents. After everything has concluded, they go home and usually write me a personal thank you letter saying, "Wow, those students were terrific, and their parents were sharp. We had a great time. Please include us the next time you have this type of event."

This is engagement at its best!

Recently, I held an all-day team strategy session at CCU. I decided I needed to go back and touch on the basics of a donor-centric operation inside of University Advancement (our fundraising team) at Colorado Christian University.

During our Strat-Op session, I presented my donor-centric cycle to the team. For their feedback, I asked if we were true to each stage in all of our operations, campaigns, and events. The team graded our efforts between 1-5, according to our intentionality, follow-through, and outcomes. This feedback process helped me to pinpoint a few areas where we had slipped and become transactional. It also helped me highlight a few areas where we had made strides in being better in our donor-centric communication, cultivation, and outcome reporting (more on this in a later chapter).

The joy of this day's eight-hour session was a quick, impromptu presentation from Matthew, our Director for Data and Donor Services. After we reviewed the donor-centric cycle and announced a short coffee break, Matthew said, "I love our donor centered philosophy, but can I show you something?" Matthew walked to the whiteboard and scribbles, "D-O-N-O-R" in a vertical fashion. Then he grabbed another color of dry-erase marker and wrote a brief descriptive beside each of the letters:

D-ialogue

O-bserve

N-otice

O-ffer (or **O**-pportunity)

R-etain

I was stunned at Matthew's creation of the acronym. He wasn't one of our Major Gift Officers but rather, an excellent data manager. I thought to myself, *if this donor-centric philosophy can go deep into the psyche of your team—including your data person, then you know your group is on the right track with your philanthropy.* It was confirmation that these practices can go deeper into your operation than just the donor facing gift officers. It can go into the DNA of your team's mindset and focused strategies – and that is any manager's satisfaction.

Be Intentional and Relational, Not Transactional

Recently, I attended a leading national philanthropic consultancy firm's weekend seminar in Chicago. The weekend's conference format was designed for a good number of the firm's "Sage on the Stage" presenters followed by table talks and breakout workshop sessions. Early in the weekend, one of these "expert" sessions was called, "Leading Indicators of Fundraising Success." The ballroom was filled and who wouldn't want to learn how to work a personal 4-to-5 step checklist which would lead to successful fundraising dollars, meet and exceeded fundraising goals, and provide an easier process of establishing future fundraising projections?

The emcee introduced the expert Fundraiser and welcomed him to the stage as the ballroom applause hit a crescendo. The fundraising expert orator jumped out from behind the podium and immediately popped up a data-driven Power-Point presentation. His presentation began, "If you want to be a successful Fundraiser you must master these task metrics." On the screen behind him he had listed this one-size fits all metric self-evaluating task table:

- 5 to 7 donor calls needed before you can make a successful ask. Notice he said phone calls, and not physical meetings.
- 3 donor visits and gift requests to make on behalf of your nonprofit organization's major donor campaign.
- 850 prospects, donor requests, and the size of your database necessary for the success of your unrestricted annual fund. He contended the size of your database would directly affect your fundraising efforts.
- Number of new Board members, or Foundation Board members, to identify and recruit during the coming year for your NPO's sustainable future. I had no idea what this metric meant.

Throughout the presentation, people were applauding and taking notes. The presenter's hour-long presentation was delivered to hundreds of national Fundraisers. Everyone was taking detailed notes and copying the "checklist graphics" from his presentation. According to this experienced speaker, if you follow all these steps, you will have fundraising success. The more I listened, my frustration increased. *Nothing* in his presentation revolved around the donor. The entire presentation was all Fundraiser-centric motives, operation(s), and myopic outcomes. When I walked out of this presentation, I was asking myself, "Where is the future of philanthropy headed? What are we teaching our future fundraising professionals? No one was talking about how to understand the donors' passions and desires."

The Winning Side of "the Ask"

The experience took me back to Lisa Greer, the multi-million-dollar philanthropist. In *Philanthropy Revolution*, Lisa laments for a more humane approach to fundraising, especially because she has been on the donor side of the equation and experienced far too many myopic and ego-driven Fundraisers. Greer pleads, "I am asking nonprofit organizations to be more upfront in their communications, more authentic in their relationships, and more transparent in their practices generally."[6] As a million-dollar donor, Greer is encouraging Fundraisers to see the donor and not their pocketbook. Instead of following some "metric," Fundraisers need to create a professional relationship.

The hour-long session I experienced in Chicago was nothing more than a pablum of "measuring transactional metrics," versus teaching the donor-centric relational skillset of learning how to be human in building intentionally relational donor engagement. A "successful ask" is not qualified with the frequency of visits, calls, or check-the-box metrics. I left that Chicago conference after a day of such sessions. As I walked out, the director of the conference pulled me aside. I said, "You have a lot of people here."

"Yes" he agreed, "and in the middle of a pandemic. It is a big boost for us as a firm. Every attendee paid a $2,500 registration fee. In addition, we received percentage kickback from the hotel for committing to the event during the pandemic."

He had just revealed his motivation for this conference. It was purely a business transaction; the exact mentality being instructed from the stage for Fundraisers to adopt when working with their

---

[6] Greer, *Philanthropy Revolution*, 27.

donors. I grabbed a coffee, returned to my hotel room, gathered my belongings, and left the weekend conference early.

What You Need is to Know

Every profession has its gurus – philanthropy is no different. For years, I have been drawn to the fundraising acumen of James M. Langley, the President of Langley Innovations. I believe Jim to be one of the foremost thinkers on donor-centric philanthropy today. He has pioneered a number of practices which hundreds of institutions in higher education, including myself, are emulating. He recently released another book entitled *The Future of Fundraising: Adapting to New Philanthropic Realities* (Academic Impressions, 2020).

In Langley's most recent book, he highlights the growing dissonance surrounding myopic fundraising lenses and a donor-centric lens. Jim succinctly draws strict comparisons between the two competing philosophies and internationalities in this side-by-side graphic:

Fundraiser-centric	Donor-centric
Crying needs	Great impact opportunities
Asking for 'donations'	Proposing a partnership
Rapidly cultivating	Brokering organizational strengths
Focuses on nonprofit organization support	Stress nonprofit organization agency
Urging donors to put funds in	Offering customized initiatives

buckets	
Asking for round number gifts	Proposals of carefully crafted budgets
Leveraging naming rights opportunities	Reserving naming rights for proven partners
Conflating gratitude with stewardship	Demonstrating institutional gratitude

Notice the distinct philosophy differences in these comparisons. Consider the effort and investment into the donor relationship the donor-centric intentionality demands. Then consider the success that this investment in human connection and developed philanthropic trust delivers over time.

Most Fundraiser-centric Major Gift Officers see a donor and their donations. The donor-centric Major Gift Officer sees a donor's passion and the donor's partnership to bring about change over time. If you want to remedy donor retention rates, facilitate the necessity to grow a committed donor roster of involved partners, and develop satisfaction in year-to-year philanthropic growth, then adjust your thinking, your heart connections, and check your ego at the door.

A Healthy Pride

As I mentioned in this book's introduction, if you can direct your philanthropy toward a donor's intentions, you will find the joy of the journey and good work. Jerry, a quality Major Gift Officer who worked on one of my previous teams at a Christian university, told me that he decided to empty himself of pride in his philanthropic work. I decided to challenge Jerry's premise and decision, asking "Jerry, do you believe pride to be sinful in every instance?"

Jerry paused, replied, "I think so. Do you agree?"

"Not so much. I do believe pride can be a vice or a virtue depending upon the circumstances, but not in every situation."

Jerry asked, "What do you mean?"

I jumped at the opportunity, "Yes, Jerry, the Bible does state that God opposes the proud but gives grace to the humble. This verse, from James 4:6, does seem straight forward."

Jerry agreed, "That's what I believe too."

"Hear me out," I said. "I believe the sin, or negative results of personal pride takes root when we stop looking to God, His providence in our fundraising efforts, and His sovereign will on display in others. This is when we start to take credit for every aspect of our success as Fundraisers."

"Right, that's my thinking ..." he said.

I continued, "We also see pride as a virtue in the Bible. Paul states in his letter to Rome (Romans 15:17), "In Christ Jesus, then, I have reason to be proud of my work for God." Notice that this pride is different. This pride depends on the foundation of God's work through me for the benefit of others."

Jerry said, "Right, there is a Fundraiser's pride and then there is a pride found in accomplishing a donor's passions in philanthropy."

I agreed and added, "I think it is very appropriate to have pride in your work, if your work is grounded in others. As Fundraisers, we need to stop being proud in a self-centered way and start being proud in a godly way. Being proud in a donor's generosity, proud of a well-trained team of Fundraisers, and proud that your NPO's mission is successful and sustainable in donors and philanthropy is a rightly adjusted pride in the work and not in yourself."

Chapter Three

First Things First: Fix the "Dirty Data"

"If your organization fails to deliver both reliable and consistent experiences, you will fail at retention. Period. The donor's level of trust allows you to move to the next, vitally important, tier of the relationship."[7] – Roger M. Craver, *Retention Fundraising*

When you accept the position as a lead Fundraiser, what is one of the assumed first tasks when beginning the job? It doesn't matter whether you are in a small organization, a medium one or a large one. Usually, the first operational decision is to consider hiring a Major Gift Officer (MGO) who can begin to work with your donors. I agree, these individuals are very important, but are they your first step? I would argue, by experience, they are not!

A vital component to create a donor-centric system and internal operations is the ability to trust, manipulate, and utilize your donor data. Frequently you'll hear a Fundraising director speak about "dirty data" episodes that cause a great amount of embarrassment for the Fundraiser and the organization. In most development or

---

[7] Roger M. Craver, *Retention Fundraising* (Medfield, Massachusetts: Emerson & Church, 2014), 29.

advancement shops, your donor data will reside in what is called a Customer Relation Management system, or your CRM. There are affordable CRM options for small shops and expensive, sophisticated CRM platforms for larger shops. In my opinion, the top two CRM products are Salesforce and Blackbaud's niche platform called Raiser's Edge. Many nonprofits say they can't afford to subscribe to a quality CRM system. I constantly counter that premise by saying, "You cannot afford not to."

If you are a small shop with 11,000 donor records that hopes to raise $850,000 a year, no matter which platform you choose, most companies will work with you on the monthly subscription cost to fit your limited budget. These CRM platforms will help you clean up your stored data and experience better success with your donor relations and fundraising practices.

I know that smaller NPOs tend to trust Excel spreadsheets to manage their vital data. Let me encourage you, depending upon Excel spreadsheets for your donor data is time consuming, clunky, dangerous, and detrimental to your fundraising efforts – not to mention being successfully donor-centric.

Every non-profit organization, whether they are small or large, needs to find a CRM that will work their donor data and your NPO's fundraising needs. I know that many smaller fundraising shops begin with a CRM program like Donor Quest. Then, as they grow, they move to a larger, more robust CRM like Blackbaud's Raiser's Edge. And again, I want to stress that the larger, more marketed CRM companies (i.e., Salesforce or Blackbaud) will work with your budget and size of operation scale. I want to emphasize that these operational systems are very sympathetic to the needs of the nonprofit organization. They desire to help you with your data and grow with you over time – if you can agree to a benchmark threshold, making this expenditure is a valuable step toward fundraising success and donor-centric realities. It will be worth the investment if you utilize the CRM properly.

At CCU, we use Raiser's Edge (Blackbaud) and we employ their mobile app (NXT) on our team's smartphones, laptops, and throughout the extended Advancement operation. As a typical practice on any day when I'm meeting donors, I will get up at 5 a.m., spend a time reading through the morning paper (yes, I still love printed newspaper), go for a two- to three-mile run. Then, as I eat my breakfast, I will review the list of donors I will be meeting with that day. I reference our last meeting and what we discussed during our time together. I reference the donor's last few gifts to see where they gave and why, and then I will look at what they want to do going forward with their philanthropic giving. My job as their donor advisor is to help them achieve these ambitions as we meet together to discuss and consider options.

The mobile app is essential. In the event that my day's agenda is running a bit late, I have the ability, on my phone, to look up Mr. and Mrs. Smith and review their information as I am driving to our appointment location – or, in the parking lot before I enter the restaurant. I want to stress again, a poor CRM process will deliver a poor donor appointment, follow-up appointment, and long-term process in building your donor-centric operation.

For example, my contact report may have noted Mrs. Smith was going to have surgery last month. When we meet, I will ask her, "How did your surgery go?" I don't pretend – or try -- to keep all of these donor details in my head.

If she asks, "Eric, how did you remember my surgery?"

I reply, "Each time we visit I keep a record and I review this information before you arrived."

Often, they will respond, "I'm amazed you took the time to record those details." Believe me, this says something important to your donor. Because I'm helping her with her giving as a donor advisor and as a professional, it's acceptable for me to show them that I am gathering and recording appropriate information about them in our data files.

If you continue to operate from old, incorrect, and dirty data, it is like navigating a new city without having GPS to give you directions and timely course detours. If your GPS on your smart phone is inoperative, you are effectively guessing on general directions and navigating without any specific geographical data to guide you. In the end, you make many wrong turns, and wind up lost. Every serious fundraising organization, whether large or small, needs a process for putting clean information into their CRM system, and a process for extracting trustworthy data to build trustworthy donor relationships.

Hire a Data Architect First!

When I was chosen to lead the fundraising effort at CCU, the first person I hired for our young team was a data architect or director of donor relations. This skillset is vital for your internal operations.

From my experience, if you hire the right person, they will stay with you for a long time, producing year-after-year value. Your donor databases carry critical information about each donor so you can build relationships with your donors throughout the years. Whether your fundraising effort is a small, medium, or large shop, it is calculated on the number of donors who have given to your organization.

For example, a very small shop would be anyone with 7,000 donor units or less. A medium shop will have up to 85,000 donor units. And a large shop has more than 225,000 units, also referred to as households.

As you keep track of this data, you want to know how connected they are to your organization, their passions, interests, their desired outcomes, yearly activities, and if they have increased in the size and frequency of their gifts.

We use several acronyms in this process. To give you an example, your database (CRM) will help you determine your LYBUNTS and SYBUNTS.

LYBUNTS is where a donor gave "last year but not this year" or SYBUNTS where a donor gave "some year but not this year." Your data architect and the director of fundraising will develop a process to clean up this data and make it current so you can relate to your lapsed donors and begin to understand who they are and why they may have lapsed. You want to find out if they are still engaged and passionate about the mission of your organization. If not, then you need to adjust them into different communication pieces, or simply remove them instead of spending time and your non-profit's money (donor dollars) to send them appeals when they are not interested. If they are deceased, you may offend some donors' families by continuing to appeal to them. If their names are spelled wrong or if they have moved or if they are retired and are no longer earning an income or if you have them listed with two children and now, they have five, it will decrease your efforts from being successful. Your effectiveness as a Fundraiser is in a direct relationship to the importance of controlling and properly using this donor data.

When you get your data clean and clear for use, then you should begin to hire qualified Major Gift Officers who can utilize your CRM. Once ready, they can actually schedule visits with your donor households and find out their current passions, and how to match those passions to the various needs of your organization to help increase a donor's satisfaction.

When I arrived at Colorado Christian University, within my first fifteen days at the helm we were having a campus event welcoming a significant number of donors. I was scheduled to be introduced to the attending donors at this event. I decided to spend a few hours ahead of the start time researching and remembering names, which is always a high wire act to perform. Before the event began, I did a quick review in our Blackbaud CRM with the RSVP list featuring the donors attending. I selected a few donor names and prepared myself to introduce myself and engage with these select university supporters. At that time, none of the donor records featured photos. As I studied the guest list, I picked out one gentleman that I felt I needed to meet (remember the donor-centric cycle).

In our donor database called Raiser's Edge, there was 25-plus years of data – which I unknowingly trusted. It was actually years of dirty data and untrustworthy contact reports. I did my best to scour through a few guest's data files, reading about past donations, a few minimally scripted previous contact reports, and the guests' vague personal information. I found Richard's file, the gentleman I wanted to meet at. I read his file thoroughly, made mental notes, and felt prepared to engage him in a warm introductory greeting that night. At the event, I recognized him from a quick reference I made searching for his Facebook page. I walked up to Richard and began my conversation with him.

"Hello Richard, my name is Eric Hogue. I am the new vice president for Advancement at CCU. It's a pleasure to meet and see you on campus tonight (handshake). Richard, may I lean upon some initial grace? Do you prefer to be called Richard or Dick?" I asked the question about his name because my father-in-law, whose name was also Richard, would always respond, "Call me Dick or little Richard." Then I also added, "By the way, how is your bride doing these days? Will she be attending with you tonight?"

Richard was nice and friendly because he knew I was new to CCU but then he said, "Eric, welcome to CCU. You will love it here. Thank you for the invitation to the nursing school social tonight. I always have been interested in CCU's School of Nursing. But ... did you know that my giving is to the theology department instead of the nursing school?" I was immediately red-faced. Our underutilized CRM database didn't contain any information about Richard or his specific interests in the theology department. The event featured a spray approach to the invitation process. Someone in Advancement had decided to invite every university donor within 20 miles of our campus. A key item of information that is also important when preparing MGOs to greet and entertain donors during a campus event.

Richard continued, "I'm pleased to attend but somewhat confused why I received the invitation."

He continued, "To your question if you can call me Dick, I'd prefer not. I like Richard because it was my father's name, and he was named after his father too. We all like Richard versus Dick." (This detail should have been in a contact report.) If Richard is comfortable to inform me about his preferred name in the first meeting, he has probably told someone else this detail, as well.

"As for my lovely wife, you're new and I am certain you have no reference. Her name was Victoria." When he used the past tense, I could image what was coming next and my heart fell to the floor. "She passed last year at this time and is with the Lord. I'm dealing with the pain of that loss as best as I can. I accepted tonight's invitation just to get out of the house and see some familiar faces here at CCU."

My first encounter with Richard was a complete train wreck due to missing, bad, and dirty CRM data. None of this critical information was in his donor file. Instead of starting a new donor relationship, I was embarrassed and hoped I could salvage this relationship for the future of the university. That night, I apologized profusely, as well as the next day in a letter I drafted and mailed from my home office. A few days later, I invited Richard to lunch, and I began the donor-centric cultivation cycle, anew.

I always remember every episode of "dirty data embarrassments." They are very painful. In fundraising, first impressions are important, especially if you are committed to a donor-centric philosophy. Each mishap with dirty data brings an anguish which never expires in that donor's experience with your organization . . . and with you as the donor advisor.

After my exchange with Richard, I knew we needed to get a data architect into our department as soon as possible. My embarrassing and eroding episode could have been avoided if the department's constituency data had been treated as a priority and designed with a donor-centric data entry philosophy and process. Our CRM recorded the various donations, years of giving, mailing addresses, phone numbers, and email addresses. We used this information for mass email announcements to list when, where, and why previous Major Gift Officers have met with donors. While maintaining this general data is important, it was not as detailed for each donor's "personal life data," something that is extremely vital.

As you consider your fundraising shop, you are probably thinking, "There is no way we can afford to purchase a customer relationship management system (CRM), nor can we spend this much time and effort gathering and recording this level of personal, granular life information for all of our donors."

My immediate response is, *"You can't afford not to!"*

Your department's *most valuable player* is your Director for Donor Services and/or Data Architect. When you begin a new job as a Fundraiser or are reorganizing a tired shop, this person should be your first hire. I've seen many other directors or vice presidents for fundraising be enticed to immediately hire a top gun Major Gift Officer, which would be a mistake from my experience. Even if your

MGO is donor-centric and excellent at fundraising, if your constituency data is dirty, you will be taking one step forward and two steps back. Eventually, this MVP MGO will either run for higher ground or begin to keep his or her own "rogue donor portfolio data" that is siloed from your systems, operation, and sustainable futures. Every nonprofit shop of any size must focus first on the quality, trustworthiness, and reliability of their donor data. Without the donor you have no means to fundraise.

This Director of Donor Services is responsible for every aspect of your CRM. They determine how to put fresh data into the system and how to extract information from the program. This person pulls together the mailing file (addresses) for any appeal letter. When our university sends our campus magazine and we determine who will receive it, the data comes from this CRM. If we decide to send an email to all of the alumni from the university, then this Director of Donor Services will schedule this electronic mailing. Over the last few years, our Director of Alumni will write the email, then our marketing department will design the digital letter and its graphics for this mailing, and they hand it over to the Director of Donor Services who puts these pieces together in a professional way to arrive in the various alumni emails. With each of these mailings, some people will unsubscribe, and this person keeps track of those changes to maintain a clean database. We personally contact each of these unsubscribing people to assure them that they wanted to unsubscribe and if so, we confirm that we will not be sending them any further digital communications and/or emails from the office.

Some emails are returned because the person has changed email addresses and not notified us. We give that information to the gift officer who will reach out to these individuals and correct our database. This process and an intentional pursuit to clarify these vital data points are examples of a constant motion to keep a clean donor database. When I meet with my team, which includes our Director of Donor Data, I often request, "I want all of our major gift officers to have at least 95% trustworthy data to use." I know our data is in a constant state of improvement so reaching 100% is impossible but striving for 95% is a very attainable goal within each fiscal campaign. The Director of Donor Data has a lot of detailed and tedious work. You need to find the right person for this position then keep them with you for a long period of time. Hire the right person and make them comfortable. Incorporate them in your team leadership processes and strategic decisions and compliment them publicly – making sure your MGOs know who has their backs when they sit before a generous donor for your NPO, charity, and mission.

I firmly believe that you will raise more funds for your organization by hiring a Director of Donor Data ahead of a qualified Major Gift Officer. You want this hire to be someone who has a great attention to detail, knows how to ask good questions, ideates on and incorporates innovation, is a forward thinker, and a good listener to the team, especially when your organization is having problems. This person must be able to listen, diagnose, and remedy fixes for your department and your colleagues. You also want an individual who is conscious of errors, committed to excellence, a truth teller, a consummate reader, and a continual learner for new training and webinars. You want someone who has godly pride in their work when they see your nonprofit increase their fundraising efforts as they make proper use of the data. This person must understand the work of the organization starts and stops at the ground floor because of their work. And you want him, or her, to find great satisfaction in their day-to-day role, processes, and the team success.

When I took over the shop at CCU there were three people. I immediately hired our Data Architect (i.e., Director of Donor Data and Services), his name was Matthew Rummel. Matthew sat in my office throughout most of my first month while we worked on getting our data into a good position. He learned that after I have a lunch with a donor, I write a detailed contact report which I give to him. I soon learned that my provided contact report's detailed information was actually a joy for Matthew to receive. Early on, I emailed him reports and he would respond by saying, "That sounds like a wonderful guy. Hey, I read this report and notice they have questions about our School of Education. I hope they get excited about where we are headed with our growing student teachers."

I was overjoyed – here was Matthew, early on the job, and he was actually reading the reports and interacting with them. When we have events on the campus or our president's dinner with our top donors, I invite Matthew to be there as a greeter when they arrive. Because he absorbs and interacts with our data, he knows our donors, and it means something to him when he shakes the hands of people where he had read the report and seen their generosity to the university. He gets a chance to say, "Hello, I'm Matthew, the Director of Donor Data and Services and I work with Eric in Advancement. I just want to say thank you for what you are doing for our mission here at CCU."

I have led my team through numerous data ideation sessions, where we determine new innovations and implement how to utilize constituency data for optimal donor-centric benefits. Now, I confess, I am not an extremely savvy tech operator. I jokingly state that I am probably only "25% *"geekified"* (an affectionate term for a high-tech acumen). Because of this reality, I trust and depend upon Matthew's work, excellence, and commitment to professionalism. Our one-on-one meetings focus on what we want from the data, how we need to input this data, and how this data supports our intentionality in being donor-centric Fundraisers.

Nonprofit organizations (NPOs) love to boast about large numbers of "people in our database." The number of donors means nothing in the scope of donor-centric relations and successful philanthropy. If you do not have a real relationship with a person in your database, then they are not an active partner -- or donor -- or passionate about your organization's mission. I constantly ask my team to shrink their portfolios and reduce the number of general donors in the database. The CRM's donor data should feature three general high-level segmentations of the thousands of collected names:

(1) Portfolio Donors,

(2) Partner, Prospects, and Annual Donors, and the

(3) General Population.

Like anything else, shrinking the database creates sincere donor-centric connections and better relationships.

Contact Reports

One example stemming from numerous portfolio meetings is the practice of creating extensive contact reports. In this aspect of fundraising practices, I go against the trend.

I prefer long and detailed contact reports.

These reports are intentional, not just factual. They should feature a donor's interests, experiences, emotions, and desired outcomes. - scaffolding narrative about each of your donors, their passion(s), and your time together. These contact reports build your present fundraising, your future fundraising, and your legacy for the future of fundraising for your organization and your committed philanthropic partners in the success of the mission's cause, impact, and outcomes. The combination of the personally crafted "portfolio and contact report" is each donor advisor's secret sauce.

A personal contact report provides a written record of a visit and other meaningful interactions with a donor (or constituent) that substantially enhances the understanding of the donor's passions, desires, and philanthropic impact and outcomes. A real contact report is not (just) a playbook, or a pithy review of meetings topics, it needs to be a detailed diary of donor discovery.

Be Like Netflix

On the anniversary of each donor's first gift to CCU, we rotate a select survey for our philanthropic partners to learn of their donor experience and philanthropic preferences. We do this online, in the mail, or it could be a text link. We are looking for feedback and updates – even changes in the donor's personality and desired impact(s). I write a cover letter and ask them to take a survey which should take about fifteen minutes. The cover letter points out the survey will be useful to us as an organization but also to them as they are a generous donor to the university. The survey is a tool to capture updated changes in their life. Normally it begins, "You made a $50 gift to CCU on December 15, 1978." We add some facts in the letter about what the cost of milk was in 1978. After these fun facts, I remind them that it is the anniversary of their first gift. "Do you mind if we get caught up on life's journeys, so we communicate in an appropriate way for you?" Matthew, our Director of Donor Data and Services, enjoys creating and sending out these donor surveys – again, he is a part of the process and the success.

We live in an era where technology, social media, and internet activities have welcomed users to a world of digital lead generation, search engine optimization, and digital media accounts that provide behavioral, preference, and demographic data recall. Because of this technology, social media knows you, your friends, and your interests. Maybe this technology knows you better than you do. I believe the goal of every donor-centric database is to be "somewhat prescriptive" versus "hopefully predictive." If we really want to meet, discover, identify, and engage our donors, a robust and strategic CRM platform and operation is vital.

Netflix is one of the best examples of this type of working system. My wife and I love to watch movies, documentaries, and sitcoms on Netflix. I love to log onto Netflix and the assigned "avatar characters" for me and my wife appear for specific viewer selection. When I select my avatar, it suggests sorted viewing options prescribed for me.

Netflix will offer my past views, my most favorite documentary genres, and recommend new programs that I may enjoy. Netflix's system knows me personally and knows my favorite viewing options. Because of previous detailed and stored "viewer contact reports," Netflix is wonderfully *viewer-centric*.

From Netflix's web home page, it states, "As a business is a subscription-based model that, over time, personalizes your membership and makes appropriate recommendations, Netflix helps its members find the shows they want to watch and will enjoy." It's as if Netflix took a page from a donor-centric philanthropic process. Every Fundraiser and philanthropic shop should program their CRM donor database, contact report processes, and each MGO's assigned portfolio with the same manner and intentionality.

Whenever you access Netflix services, their recommendation system strives to help you, the viewer, to find a show or movie to enjoy with minimal effort. Netflix estimates the likelihood that you will watch a particular title in their catalog based on a number of factors including:

1. Your interactions with Netflix, such as your viewing history and how you rated other viewing titles you watched and experienced.
2. Other Netflix members with similar tastes and their experiences and preferences.
3. Information about the titles, such as their genre, categories, actors, release year, that you frequently search, watch, or visit.
4. In addition to knowing what you have watched on Netflix, they will also look at information such as the time of day you

watch, the devices you are using for Netflix, and how long you watch each selection.

These pieces of data are used as personal data inputs, or viewer contact reports, that Netflix uses to process viewer *algorithms*. An algorithm is a process or set of rules to be followed in calculations for a problem-solving operation.

Every donor database, Data Architect, and gift officer needs to think and operate in this same way. I disagree with consultants who state that contact reports need to just include the simple facts and high-level agenda items during the appointment. I must be clear here *– you cannot go light on post-donor meeting contact reports and be successfully donor-centric*! In my opinion, these reports (donor journals) are better if they are lengthy and detailed about the relationship information. From donor contact reports to past donor donations, quality donor data is gathered into a donor-centric CRM database in order to create trust, intentionality, and donor algorithms. This discipline delivers legitimate contact reports, accurate donation attributions, and quality personal donor data. As the database tracks on which events each donor likes to attend, Major Gift Officers can utilize each contact report's information as an intentional algorithm toward a donor-centric processes leading to fundraising futures, process sustainability, and ultimate philanthropic success and experience(s) of each donor.

Jumpstart Cultivation

When you create your Netflix account, or add a new profile in your account, Netflix will ask you to choose a few titles that you like.

They use your offered titles to "jumpstart" your recommendations. Once you start watching movies, or shows, on Netflix, the titles you actually choose and enjoy will begin to "supersede" those initial preferences. As you continue to watch over time, the titles you watched more recently begin to outweigh titles you watched in the past in terms of driving your recommendations.

This is another great model for programming your CRM database process and systems. When you welcome a new donor into your organization, ask them how they would like you to communicate with them. Ask them if they prefer text, email, phone, or snail mail letters. Ask them how they would like to be addressed for their salutations on letters. Do they prefer surnames and honorary titles and academic degrees? Ask them which areas of your organization capture their interest and why. Discover which types of events they would like to attend and then invite them to attend. In essence, jumpstart your cultivation process with donor-centric questions to better understand the donor.

Over time, just like Netflix, these initial preferences and expressions will be homed in and replaced with a deeper, more connected relationship.

Database Anniversary Survey

Each time you visit Netflix, the company receives feedback and continually retrains their algorithms to improve the accuracy of their prediction of what you're likely to watch. Netflix data, algorithms, and computation systems continue to sample from viewers and feed into their systems to deliver updated recommendations to viewers.

Without any fanfare, fundraising shops should do the same. One of the best ways for this annual housekeeping is to use a "CRM anniversary date" for the calendar year. On this internally determined annual date, your Director for Donor Services and/or Data Architect offers a donor database survey to a determined number of your active donors.

This designed tool helps you survey your selected donor segmentation once a year. Ask for categorized feedback and updated (or confirmed) data. You can easily ask donors if they are receiving appropriate communications, invitations, and president/director communications. If they attended a particular event, you would learn how they enjoyed the event, or not. You will know if they received timely responses thanking them for their generous donations. You can also ask if they have any suggestions, desire to volunteer, or invite friends to the cause and mission of your NPO. Here's some of the data you will want to collect:

1. Correct spelling of first and last names residing in the donor household.
2. Donors' birthdays (ages) and wedding anniversary date (and any previous spouses).
3. The current and past employment for the household income-earners.
4. Contact data: cell phone numbers, hard line residential numbers, office, or workplace phone number(s), email addresses, and the correct (or desired) physical address(es).
5. A note on the donors' preferred method of communication.

6. Date of the donors' first gift to your NPO and any/all notes associated with the gift(s).
7. A cumulative total of your donors' gifts to your NPO.
8. An updated photo of the couple, donor, and/or household members.
9. Children and grandchildren information, number, names, and ages.
10. Any planned gifts expressed to your NPO. And any written and expressed estate or trust documents.
11. (sensitive) If you have wealth screened your donor(s), provide the most recent report in their confidential file (update this process every three years).
12. Reviewed and updated historical contact reports.

These are a dozen of the most desirable data points to begin a donor advisor relationship. On a few occasions I have taken copies of the donor's historical contact reports which were often completed by my predecessor(s). During our initial meeting, or during a second appointment in the discovery stages, I ask the donor if the reports express an accurate representation of the meeting's dialogue, content, and conversation. Before I present any printed reports for review, they are redacted and edited. The results of this practice have been stellar. Each time I have reviewed previous, historical contact reports, the donors responded favorably with additional details, emotions, and mission passions.

For the annual survey, there is no need to invent something from scratch. I have adapted surveys from wealth management organizations such as Baird, Charles Schwab, and Merrill Lynch Wealth Management. If your goal is to be a trusted donor advisor for your generous donors in your portfolio who are giving to your NPO, I have no hesitation to adapt an instrument from a financial profession that mandates a robust CRM system, trustworthiness, and personal relationship featuring high integrity.

Redesign Job Titles

You may find this section to be remedial – I guarantee you it is not. Your staff job titles are another form of data to be considered. Obviously, team titles don't carry much weight internally, but I believe they carry a tremendous amount of meaning externally, especially to your donors. Each time I cringe when I am introduced before a crowd, or when I am asked, "What's your title at CCU?" When I say Vice President for Advancement, they immediately followed up with. "So, what does that mean?"

Our internal meaningless job titles are not dirty data. But this data can easily create a good amount of donor dissonance. Over the past three years I have understood donors prefer a Fundraiser's succinct job title. More importantly, donors want to see themselves in the various philanthropic job titles.

Recently I wrote my entire staff's job titles on the whiteboard in my office. I asked myself, "If I were a prospective donor would I know who to call and what their job actually is in Advancement?" At CCU we had two MGOs titled "Senior Major Gift Officers." If you're a donor and you want to make a single, generous, annual fund gift of $250 to the CCU Fund, you read the titles. As you read the titles on the Advancement web page, you run across our "Senior Major Gift Officers." After discussing this issue with a few tenured CCU donors, I'm convinced a majority of donors are paralyzed when the job title does not relate to them. The donor ponders, "Is a $250 gift a major gift?" If the conclusion that the Senior Major Gifts Officer is not the right pathway, she searches further and eventually makes an online donation without connecting to anyone in my shop.

I decided to redesign my department job titles. I want every current and prospective donor to see themselves in every one of my staff's job titles. After a few weeks of consideration, I changed a number of titles into:

Former Title	New Title	Donor's Eyes
Director of Foundations and Scholarships	Director for Strategic Philanthropy	Most grants and scholarships involve donor-centric strategies
Data Architect	Director for Donor Services and Data Architect	The donor feels welcome to make a call and to inquire of a recent gift
Senior Major Gifts Officer	Senior Director for Donor Relations	Removes the dissonance of major gifts, welcomes a relationship
Annual Gifts Officer	Director for Annual Funds	For donors who desire to give

		annually and enter a specific donor community of giving, this is easier to comprehend
Event Coordinator	Donor Event Catalyst	Who doesn't like the word "catalyst" in a title? Safe to include it around events
Vice President of University Advancement	Vice President of Philanthropy and Donor Relations	When this title is offered it is easily understood. Most repeat the tile and say, "so you're the guy in charge."

Returning to First Things First

In the Bible, Jesus went through Samaria and met the woman at the well. There was a lot of push for Jesus not to travel this direction. The disciples asked Jesus, "Why go through Samaria?"

"Because there is someone I need to meet," Jesus answered. He knew that he would meet the woman at the well. When they get to the well, a Samaritan woman approached, and Jesus begins to speak with her.

The woman spoke with Jesus and from the conversation, she understood Jesus was the promised Messiah. With her understanding she is embarrassed and feels guilty because she says, "You really don't know me."

Jesus says, "I do know you and the man you are with and the previous five men."

This Bible story shows Jesus had a sincere characteristic of meeting people intentionally. With our fundraising, we must be sincere in meeting people intentionally. When Jesus met someone for the first time or over a period of time, he was focused on the data of their lives. With this data, Jesus could understand the algorithm of their lives and their human condition.

I would hope with the work we do in philanthropy to change lives, that we would treat donors the same way. While we can't equal deity, we are told to be Christ-like. I believe being donor-centric is being Christ-like. The process starts with trustworthy, successful, and attributable donor data employed through a donor-centric philanthropy; something we will continue to describe as we journey in this book.

Chapter Four

Emerging Donor Personalities

"Lincoln is the leanest, lankest, most ungainly mass of legs, arms, and hatcher-face ever strung upon a single frame. He has most unwarrantably abused the privilege which all politicians have of being ugly."[8] – Doris Kearns Goodwin, *Team of Rivals*

I carry a simple bound notebook which I use almost every day for fundraising. I use this notebook as my professional journal. I recommend every Fundraiser create and maintain a personal fundraising journal or a series of moleskins. As you are intentional about being donor-centric, you should keep a written record of insights into donors and their philanthropic personalities. People change over time and nothing is set in stone about people and their personalities; you want to track and understand the core of their "personality for giving." As your work becomes more donor-focused, you will notice some distinctive donor personalities, and if you're

---

[8] Doris Kearns, *Team of Rivals* (New York, NY: Simon & Schuster, 2005), 47.

blessed to work with certain donors over time, you will notice slight changes and adjusted characteristics surrounding their personalities.

When I ask my team if they are using their professional journal, I often discover that some of them have slacked off from making entries. I quickly encourage them to get back on the wagon. When you keep personal notes (not contact reports), you will reference entries that state discoveries such as, "I never thought Henry would give to a crowd funding page. He told me about giving $5,000 through a crowd funding page for the mission field that he learned about at his church. Henry is 78 years old." In my journal I prompted myself during our next appointment to discover how Henry made the digital platform donation. I learned Henry's grandson helped him make the donation. He told me how much he enjoyed the experience and the impact of making that gift and offered that he may do it again in the future. Upon this revelation, I added Henry to all of our giving day emails and communication(s). At 78 years of age, Henry found the process as invigorating as the donation – something I wanted to experience with him.

Journaling gives you a way to document interesting experiences, growing relationships, and make notes about constant discoveries. It helps you discover trends and how they are tied to the donor culture. It is important to have a chronological journal. In 2010, I discovered a shift in donor personalities and the discovery came from consistently writing in my professional journal. Post-recession in 2007-09, donors in 2010 were determined to kick-start their giving rapidly and with an intention toward an immediate impact and outcome for their favorite NPOs.

I was at William Jessup University when our Advancement department was one of the first universities in the nation to offer a completely online digital fundraising campaign. We called and trademarked it "Give:24." At that time no other university had operated a live, single-day, completely online fundraising event – long before any new what a crowd funder or Go Fund Me application was. The goal was to attract new and younger donors to the university's annual campaign. Give:24 featured a simple donor message: "Give $24 within 24 hours and get 24 of your friends to do the same." We had a goal of raising $50,000 from 200 new or lapsed donors. Instead, the program welcomed over 350 donors and raised almost $100,000. My team's collegial efforts led to Jessup's first one-day, completely online, giving campaign. In my journal, I noted the excitement and ability to immediately report back to welcome and thank new donors so they could experience the excitement and the impact of the day. To this day, William Jessup University operates Give:24 each spring to great success and amazing new donor cultivation.

In my journaling, I am intentional to review my experiences, noting what is new, what is innovative and how donors are thinking and acting differently. Because of my journaling (again, these are not contact reports), I learn how emerging personalities are expecting a different type of communication and connection from me and the university. I have often referenced my journal notes stating, "What we used to do isn't working anymore, so it needs to stop. We need to change and remodel our systems, processes, and data." From these notes, comments, and musings, my teams have innovated and implemented numerous donor-centric processes at WJU and CCU. It keeps you, your team, and your department on the cutting edge of innovation, technology, and forward-looking strategies.

This journal is not a contact report about specific donors,[9] but it is more reflective and features a bigger practicum picture. I'm writing about the trends, discoveries, and peculiarities. Wayne Gretzky, a Hall of Fame professional NHL hockey player, when asked about playing the game and being ahead of the defenders on the ice said, "I don't skate to where the puck is. I skate to where the puck is going." As we write in our professional journal about our experiences, we are trying to see where philanthropy is going – where philanthropic personalities are going – even changing.

In 2011, I took a course called "The Basics of Philanthropy from Indiana University/Purdue University (IU/PUI) attending a cohort in San Francisco. My instructor for the initial day was Stephen, a professor at IUPUI and former vice president for advancement at a state institution. Stephen stated, "As you work with donors, you will begin to understand their personalities." He referred to the early 1990's philanthropic traditionalists who categorized donor styles (personalities) with a rigid and strict template. Russ A. Prince and Karen M. File highlighted these categories in their book, *The Seven Faces of Philanthropy* (Published by Jossey-Bass, 1994).[10] Prince and File described seven traditional giving characteristics of philanthropic

---

[9] Jason McNeal, Ph.D., *Writing Meaningful Contact Reports: A Handbook for Fundraisers* (Academic Impressions, Denver, CO., 2019), a very useful book for contact report building.

[10] Russ Alan Prince and Karen Maru File, *The Seven Faces of Philanthropy* (Jossey-Bass Publishers, San Francisco, CA., 1994), 13-17.

personalities which they labeled "communitarians, dynasts, altruists, repayers, socialites, investors, and the devout." These seven characteristics continue to be utilized within a traditional philanthropic practice.

Here is a brief description of the seven traditional philanthropic personalities from Prince and File:

Communitarians. This donor gives because they have a particular mission or purpose. As an example, Michelle gives because she is familiar with the cause and mission of a local organization. She understands the effect of her philanthropy and enjoys its impact. Michelle and Paul, her husband, may serve on the local board of directors, help steward the nonprofit organization, as well as engage her business for the benefit of the local neighborhood or community. She believes active philanthropy is good because it helps her community and supports her NPO's mission. In addition, she encourages others to join her in supporting this local cause. Her giving is controlled to measurable local outcomes.

Project C.U.R.E is an NPO that originated in Denver, Colorado, which sends donated medical supplies and equipment to under-resourced countries. A number of donors give to this organization because it is local, knowing they will never travel to a developing country themselves. These motivated donors cannot travel internationally, but they will commit to supporting Project C.U.R.E., as well as invest their time by visiting the NPO's warehouse to help sort through the various medical supply donations to get them prepared to be shipped overseas. For Communitarians, they invest their time, talent, and treasure for the mission of the NPO and the personal connection they receive from a community of fellow philanthropists with the same passion and the same time (volunteering) effort.

Dynasts. These donors typically inherit their wealth. If you lived in Southern California and met the Thompsons, people would say the Thompson's came from old money. In the late 50s, the Thompson family bought a home on several acres of land in Orange County and paid off their mortgage. The parents passed this property on to their kids and in the past 70-plus years that asset has appreciated from $250,000 to $3.4 million. When the children inherited this property and the family business, they wisely invested their wealth into Silicon Valley and the tech industry. Today the Thompson family, with their inherited property, family business, trust, and their wise investments, is worth between $50 and $75 million.

Chuck, one of the Thompson's great grandsons, became philanthropically active because he believed it was the duty and desired legacy of his portion of the Thompson family. When his parents passed, they left him and his wife the balance of their family estate and the operation of the family foundation. Chuck quickly navigated to duty and philanthropic involvement, which mimicked his parents' passions. He created a donor advised fund (DAF) for his current salary assets in addition to the operation of his family's sizeable charitable foundation. Chuck, his wife, and his kids love social interaction and the influence that socialization offers them as major philanthropists. Their family has always been involved in giving and they believe they are expected to support various nonprofits regionally, even nationally. The Thompson family embraced the dynasts philanthropic personality. They believed they were blessed, they had the means to bring about great outcomes and impact(s), and they were intentional about making their philanthropy make a difference.

Altruists. These donors embody the perception of the selfless donor. Don gives out of personal generosity and sincere empathy to urgent or failing causes. He almost always wants to remain anonymous. Altruists like Don believe there is a moral good to giving -- that it is good for their personal moral development to care for others as a human being and citizen. Don understands the business side of the nonprofit organization, but he gives from his own personal wealth because of the opportunity from the NPO and the plight of its recipients from its cause. Don works behind the scenes and is usually not a board member. When he attends events, Don desires to remain out of sight and in the back of the room. To show his active interest, Don takes the Fundraisers' phone calls, reads the NPOs publications, and occasionally sends a letter of encouragement (with a donation). As long as Don feels his connection and experiences the mission success, he is a lifelong donor and an eventual planned gift prospect. These types of donors want to give without any recognition or credit. They continue to give because this experience of giving changes them, and they are on a journey.

At William Jessup University, we worked with a ministry called Feed My Starving Children. Our students would volunteer to work in their warehouse and pack bags of food which would be shipped around the world. They packed eight different containers of wheat, rice, minerals, and beans. Using scoops, the students would measure the ingredients into bags, which were placed on pallets and shipped to international locations. The warehouse experience was designed to be done with your graduating class, local church group, Bible study, or your collegial office staff.

During one week, these groups would package a million meals.

I took my department and we worked together for an hour putting the meal bags together. At the next table were nine people from a real estate company. After our shift, everyone went over and received a soft drink for refreshment. I began to speak with Daniel, the CEO of the real estate company. He said, "I bring my team to this event every year. I believe in the mission, but the experience does a great deal of work for the comradery for my team. I bring these folks because it changes them." For the altruistic personality, the end and the means (the process) is equally important. Altruistic donors do not want the attention, they want the experience – both philanthropically, by volunteering and being a part of the process.

Repayers. Lori is philanthropic because she is, first and foremost, a breast cancer survivor and a beneficiary from the Jimmy V Foundation, a nonprofit named for Jimmy Valvano, a legendary basketball coach who helped to launch the foundation for cancer research before his death due to cancer. Today it is one of the leading institutions of cancer research and Lori recognizes she benefited from this foundation. While Lori does not have great wealth, she is overflowing with gratitude and generosity. She had a double mastectomy, and her cancer is now in remission. She reflects this appreciation through her recurring donations to the Jimmy V Foundation. As a typical repayer, Lori views her gifts to the Jimmy V

Foundation as paying back to those who gave to her through cancer research.

There are many examples of repayers such as college scholarship recipients who create scholarship funds, or health facility donors who were treated in a specific health care facility. The pay it forward theme in society comes from these repayers. Also, repayers exist in the church through specific outreach programs, because they heard about the truth, grace, and love of Jesus Christ.

Socialites. These are the donors who like to be seen. They enjoy dressing up and going to dinners and events downtown. These donors find social functions which benefit a nonprofit organization. Socialites are locally connected where they leverage social relationships to bring about community changes. These donors like to network and connect. Often these events feature live auctions, and they actively participate in these auctions. They enjoy the bidding for the different items. They attend five course meals at these events and these donors are going to mention their gift for $150,000 because they want the recognition for their philanthropy. They are outspoken about it because they want others in the room to give in the same way. I've been to a number of these events where they have silent auctions, and the donors get into a bidding war over items which helps the mission of the nonprofit to raise funds. These donors tend to support the arts, education, and religious nonprofits.

Investors. These donors are affluent, and they tend to give with one eye on the NPO cause and the other on personal tax relief and estate consequences. Investors desire to work with the NPO to incorporate campaigns that feature planned gift vehicles, annuities, and future tax benefits with immediate NPO results. Investors donate to a wide range of NPOs, hoping to layer their tax breaks and benefits. Many investors gravitate to planned gift vehicles where the donor, the charity, and the outcomes all mutually benefit from the gift(s). By creating a charitable remainder trust (CRT), the donor can offer a piece of property to an NPO-assigned CRT. The property can be sold to a buyer through the established CRT, giving the donor a break of capital gains tax and any income tax. In exchange, the NPO receives all of the liquid assets from the CRT property donations and its ensuing sale. In the end, it's an investment opportunity for the donor, the buyer, and – ultimately – the NPO. Investor personalities are growing in popularity and within the philanthropic population.

Devout. These donors feature a religious, moral passion in their philanthropy. If a donor is in this category, they believe in the biblical concept of tithes and offerings. In addition, they give to support missions and missionaries. Years ago, people came to Christ through ministries like Campus Crusade for Christ, now known as CRU, or Billy Graham Evangelistic Association. Initially they gave to these ministries as a repayer but eventually they switched into a devout evangelical who gave to the ministry. They believe God has called them to participate. Their resources come from God, and they steward their wealth for the glory of God's name and kingdom. The devout channel their giving to their church, parish, and/or synagogue, or para-church ministries and educational organizations at a rate of nearly 95% of their philanthropy.

Today These Personalities Have Changed

As I mentioned earlier, beginning in 2010 there was a shift in these personalities. Fundraising with social media came into play with crowdfunding, marketed digital platforms, and innovative fundraising processes, some embracing transactional (non-donor-centric) cultivations. Additionally, there were new efforts surrounding the environment, the earth's sustainability, and the role of creation care responsibility. This period began with the individual use of platforms such as the "Go Fund Me" platform. Philanthropic innovation, cultural shifts, and extended capital campaigns began to change donor personalities. This transformation gave the donor an opportunity to give, experience the process, and provide a look behind the philanthropic curtain – learning, first-hand, ethical and unethical practices in fundraising. Through these tools, cultural shifts, and donor experiences, many donors made a personality shift, and it was as though a light bulb of awareness turned on in their giving situations.

This philanthropic transition has created what I have labeled "emerging donor personalities." After years of traditional labels that, at times, ignored a donor's personality and specific passions, today's philanthropic landscape has emerging donor personalities that must be understood, recognized, and cultivated distinctively.

The best example of this cultural change is crowdfunding and Go Fund Me pages. A distinct group of people, rather than a cultivated group of donors, can have an immediate impact with their giving. A small group of like-minded people – maybe a youth group, or a neighborhood card club, can orchestrate their collective giving toward a water well in South Africa, or they can raise money for a community member who has been injured in a traffic accident. These philanthropic changes, digital and localized, have offered donors an experience of control, impact, and measured outcomes. It's a game changer in the philanthropic world whether you recognize it or not.

This philanthropy shift period also welcomed millennials and Gen Z to the party. These younger, more immediate, and localized philanthropists didn't have to donate through the church, the NPO, or the national foundation to have a satisfying experience of helping, supporting, and measuring impact.

The church is still trying to comprehend this shift. Giving to the local church dropped off as these younger donors saw they could go direct through a web page, smart phone app or a crowd funder page to impact their world with their giving instead of '*the old way of giving through the local church.*' As these young demographics grow older (more mature) and they begin to increase their income, wealth, and their giving, Fundraisers will need to relate to their emergent philanthropic personalities to be successful in raising the necessary NPO philanthropy going forward.

With the COVID-19 pandemic, many elements of philanthropy continue to change. Some of my portfolio donors were calling me and asking how the university and students were doing with the pandemic. These individuals have shifted their giving from long-term interests to something with a more immediate impact and student measured outcomes. The shift in 2010 to 2015 combined with the 2020 pandemic has changed the personalities of donors and moved them away from these traditional seven faces into new, discoverable, emerging philanthropic personalities.

While attending a IUPUI conference in San Francisco, the presenter put the outdated, traditional, seven personalities on a slide and proclaimed they are not philanthropic investors any longer. He said, "If someone is going to invest, they choose to be active in the stock market first, not philanthropy." I wrote this quotation in my journal and personally challenged this statement immediately. With all that has transpired and happened on a local, national, and international stage, I believe today's donors are significantly different than they were in 2000, 2005, or 2010. They are asking investor-like questions surrounding their philanthropy.

We are building a new science center at CCU, and a couple of our lead donors have asked me: "If we build the science center, how many new students will enroll at CCU because of this new center and its coursework?"

I responded with the feasibility research that reports an additional 350 to 400 new students will enroll at CCU because of this program's new building.

Their next question is "If I give you a million dollars for the science center, will that help you get fifty or seventy-five of those new students each year?"

I offer, "Closer to fifty students because we will need to receive a few million to help with scholarships, the endowment, and faculty hires within the program, and then to meet the growth of the School of Science and Engineering at CCU."

The final question will be, "How does that lead to the sustainability of the university?" And there it is – this question is an investor question. Today's donors are thinking as investors saying: "If

I give you a million for the building with others adding to the campaign total, what is expected enrollment? What are your tuition costs and how will this build and deliver sustainability to the program and the university? Will this help the School of Science and Engineering become a magnet program nationally?" Those types of questions are from a venture investor philanthropist. They are focused on the need, the outcome, and the impact – as well as in the return on investment!

During the last ten years, several of these "Emerging Philanthropic Personalities" are growing more prevalent. During the next decade the majority of older donors, whose generosity has sustained and built our charities for years, will start to decline. Nonprofit organizations will not be able to continue to solicit younger donors in the same way they have cultivated traditional donor personalities. These emerging personalities of donors will forge new philanthropic realities and demand more from their philanthropic participation – and every fundraising professional better be ready for what is fast approaching.

Emerging donor personalities will demand that the NPO and the professional Fundraiser change and adapt with them, embracing their new (emergent) philosophies, cultivation processes, desired outcomes and impact(s), and the practices each fundraising shop employs. These younger demographic personalities will make up the majority of the emerging philanthropic era. Future NPOs will no longer be able to funnel the donors to their "needs based" fundraising cases and campaigns. These emerging philanthropists will force the NPOs to adjust to their donor-centric (specific) priorities, passions, and interests. I am warning you, if you and your NPO do not adjust, the donors will find another organization that will.

As million-dollar philanthropist Lisa Greer boldly proclaimed, "I'm convinced that people aren't giving as much because the process is fundamentally flawed, unproductive, and often downright unpleasant. If today's fundraising tactics actually preclude connection, instead of fostering it, will people continue to give?"[11] She is speaking as a donor, and it's best we listen to what she is saying to us – for us. I believe major donors will continue giving, but these emerging philanthropists are looking for organizations they can partner with, increase, and gain sustainable realities which bring about the necessary changes for the good of mankind, culture, and the world. These personalities are usually younger – 45 years old and younger – and fall into the demographic categories: Millennials, Gen Z, and (still) younger Baby Boomers. These donors are the ones decidedly moving away from the traditional seven personalities and toward what I have labeled and describe as the "new emerging donor personalities:"

> ➢ Venture Philanthropist
> ➢ Entrepreneur Philanthropist
> ➢ Grunge Philanthropist

A **Venture Philanthropist** is a donor who is drawn to philanthropic investment risks. This donor completely understands that her donations will be "invested" into an emerging new or

---

[11] Greer, *Philanthropy Revolution*, 56.

expanding NPO mission project(s) in which there is a substantial element of possible failure.

It's similar to an investment made in Tesla ten years ago. That was an optimistic, intentional, high-risk investment, but the investor believed people were going to migrate to electric cars. This type of venture donor is futuristic.

Venture philanthropy is happening more and more frequently. I had lunch with Sam who historically contributed to major capital campaigns at the university, such as the $42 million campaign to build the Armstrong Center at Colorado Christian University. As we met, Sam asked about the "next phase" of capital campaign structures to be built for CCU programs. He had heard a short narrative about a building for the School of Science and Engineering. Sam said he would fulfill his pledge to the Armstrong Center campaign, but he wanted to immediately prepare a larger donation for the Science Center. Sam asked, "Do you have a design on the Science Center?"

"No." I responded.

"What is the square footage and how many labs?" Sam pressed.

I was caught off-guard, "We don't have any of this information yet." I was thinking this conversation was headed nowhere fast. He inquired about enrollment and a couple of other aspects but, at the time of our appointment, I had no feasibility details or data for him.

Sam continued, "Do you have any current science students on campus?"

"Yes, we have about 80 students."

"Where are they meeting?"

"They are campus homeless (meaning no designated building) and meet in classrooms that aren't really labs, but we're doing something make-shift in the interim."

When Sam heard that last phrase, he said, "That's where I want to give. I want to give so you can think about designing the building, enrolling the students, and to impact the culture."

This conversation with Sam happened at the height of the pandemic. This is how CCU's academics focused on fitness, kinesiology, nursing, elderly care, engineering (brick and mortar and digital), pre-med and virtual media all gained lift.

Sam continued "I believe science has enough atheists. It's time to populate the sciences with competent, well-educated, Christians. I am willing to give to see this happen before my days are up on this earth."

At the end of our lunch, Sam promised to call next week. When he called, He wanted to make an anonymous gift of $6 million dollars to these plans. It wasn't a pledge but an outright gift. Sam gave as a venture philanthropist because one day he knows there will be a measurable outcome from his gift and a significant, even sustainable future, from his venture philanthropy.

Sam's lead gift offered immediate momentum to the campaign. After three months, fundraising was flowing into the Science Center with donors repeating Sam's original investment.

When I picked up the check from Sam, I said, "You realize I still don't have any drawings to show you."

He nodded and said, "I understand your programs are still in the idea stage."

I said, "With the pandemic, it could take us two to four years to break ground on this building and we may have a rough time raising the money to build it." He nodded again, "I realize that."

I asked a question which I normally don't ask, but I needed to know the answer, "Why are you doing this, Sam? You could have pledged the money, but you gave us the funds instead of holding on to it."

Sam said, "I want you to hold on to it, put it in your endowment and invest it and keep it within my restricted gift for the Science Center." Then he told me, "Eric. I know it's risky, but I trust you and the leadership at CCU. I believe it's a good idea and I trust you'll do it and do it well."

Sam is a venture philanthropist and offered millions of dollars for a building that would house future science, engineering, and bio-ethic studies. He also knew that at most Christian universities, the sciences can be a bit of a risky theological academic arena. Yet it didn't matter to Sam. He gave to develop the programs with hope that it will lead to greater impact and measurable outcomes for the university, our students, and our culture at large.

Venture Philanthropists Characteristics:
  - ➤ Donor has personal passion to begin a necessary program.
  - ➤ Donor believes the nonprofit needs to do this and willingly invests.
  - ➤ The research showed the organization was weak in a certain area of impact and outcomes, so this donor wants to bolster the weakness into a strength.

> The nonprofits' growth and expanded or sustainable future is in the donor's mind and intentions.
> Donor has the wealth, personal influence, clear mission-fit, and displays a "willing to risk" profile.

In my portfolio, I have nine of these individuals. They will invite me to lunch and the purpose of the entire gathering is to brainstorm innovative and risky ventures at the university for their giving.

Recently, a donor named Rick asked, "What are you doing with CCU online?"

I answered, "Through the work of our College of Adult and Graduate Studies, we have nearly 9,000 enrolled in our online campus for undergraduate, graduate, and even doctoral programs."

Rick asked a series of questions such as, "How can we increase this enrollment? How is faculty pay handled?" Then he also asked, "What could we do to increase the reach and scope of this platform nationally?"

"There has been a discussion surrounding a partnership effort." I replied. "Like a franchise."

With enthusiasm he said, "We could call it a franchise lease." I am thinking that the concept would take CCU's online platform and curriculum and let other partnering universities brand it for themselves and their program enrollment. He initially suggested that CCU could receive 65% of the tuition the franchisees would charge, allowing the franchisees to keep 35% of the funds. What Rick embraced was a focused entrepreneurial philanthropist personality, a strict business model embedded in philanthropic ideation. This venture would help students graduate faster with less student loan debt. This innovative venture model is good for the student, good for the sustainable mission of CCU, and good for universities who don't have the upfront revenue to build an online model from the ground up. It is a cultural win-win-win for all parties.

Then Rick asked, "What if I invested three or four million dollars? Could you hire a sales team to offer this to four or five Christian universities? You, as the lead franchising university, would be making increasing your bottom line and helping other Christian universities increase their bottom lines and sustainability."

I'm seeing more and more Venture philanthropists like Rick. They are philanthropic risk takers, they are "needle-movers," but mostly frenetic Christian philanthropic partners willing to engage in a mission-focused partnership.

An **Entrepreneur Philanthropist** is a donor who wants to partner with a nonprofit for operational revenue growth. An entrepreneur is a promoter. He is a person who has experience in organizing and operating financial growth, while taking on greater than normal financial risk to gain a return on investment. The entrepreneur understands the partnership, but this donor is going to help the nonprofit organization to succeed. They are not only giving their donation but also their time and energy with the gift.

Marvin is a national multi-purpose real estate developer. As a Christian, for every one of his multi-family developments, Marv tries to hire a Christian manager. This employee not only manages the complex but ministers to the families who live there. For our CCU online program, Marv has asked if we might offer a certificate program or even an undergraduate program or a master's program for managing multi-family real estate properties. He understands that within the program we can embed not only Bible training and counseling sessions, but techniques for sharing the Good News about Jesus (the Gospel) and allowing these facility managers to love on their tenants and neighbors. Marv also encouraged our program to fully train the managers in accounting, taxes, covenant codes, and other aspects of the real estate management business.

Recently I was on a conference call with Marvin and our Dean of the School of Business Online. During the conversation, Marv offered to write the curriculum, lecture to the classes, even operate Zoom sessions from the various properties that he owns. Students could do their capstone project or their dissertation with the data that Marv could provide from one of his properties in St. Louis, Chicago, or Portland. In addition, Marv would donate an initial $2.5 million to launch the program. Marvin is an entrepreneur philanthropist. He is offering his company, donating money, his data, and even sweat equity for lecturing. This project is a risk, but he is involved day to day with this entrepreneurial partnership.

In addition, Marv said if his managers enroll, he will give them scholarships and when they graduate, he will give them a different title and additional pay because they have been trained through CCU. "I want my managers to learn how to manage the facility with all of the business procedures, yet when they go to work every day, minister to the people who live there."

Here's a second example of an entrepreneur philanthropist. Mr. and Mrs. Mathews own commercial and private real estate properties. Over the years, they systematically installed leading solar, renewable, and environmentally safe utilities and appliances in all of their apartments. They believed in the new technology so much, the Mathews invested into environmental IPO companies absorbing nice investment returns and personal asset growth. The Mathews had a daughter who enrolled at CCU as a freshman. She drove a new EV (electronic vehicle) and stored her car on the CCU campus and in her assigned residence hall parking lot.

The Mathews asked for a luncheon to discuss the possibility of placing two new EV charging stations nearby their daughter's campus residence. Her EV car takes close to 45-minutes to fully charge. The Mathews offered to donate two stations and to cover three years of upkeep and maintenance. They wanted to satisfy their daughter's charging dilemma and also seed, as they called it, an opportunity for future EV growth and non-traditional revenue (NTR) for the university. I thanked them for their donation and their interest in other CCU students, as well as CCU's creation care future as environmental stewards.

I probed, "What does 'seeding future NTR' look like in your expressed generosity?"

The Mathews were happy to describe, "We are Christians who care about the environment. We believe God told us to have dominion over the earth and to care for it. We believe that our donation for two EV charging stations will turn into more – and at different campus locations."

I agreed, "This is a wonderful example and student incentive. We are thankful for your trust and your gifts. I firmly believe more and more Christian college students are environmentally conscientious and concerned, but how does this turn into non-traditional revenue for the university?"

They replied, "Eric, we believe that if you create a welcoming student body toward creation care and environmental issues, you will also attract the companies that innovate, design, and sell these products. In fact, we are heavily invested in one of these willing companies." The Mathews are a family of entrepreneur philanthropists. They wanted their daughter to have an on-campus EV charger and for others to have the same opportunity. In addition, they had "outside of the box" thinking attached to their donation. The Mathews believed the original EV charging station would attract more students to drive EVs and to enroll at CCU. Over time they foresaw that for profit EV companies would invest in CCU and provide CCU a line of NTR that benefits the university, its prized students, and future funding.

The original EV charging stations have been installed. They have attracted a fair amount of student use and interest. The Mathews recently visited with me and agreed to three-pledges to build four to five new EV charging stations on campus in association with the construction of the next two academic buildings. As for the external EV companies, as of yet, nothing has materialized, but innovative NTR conversations with these companies and federal foundations are underway.

Entrepreneur Philanthropist Characteristics

➤ The Donor sees opportunity over minimal risk.

➤ Donors are personally involved and want to "partner" with the nonprofit.

➤ Donors will first "wait and see," then start the effort and see if it grows in support. If it does, they usually recommit to further donations.

➤ These are not usually new programs, but innovative diversity, or a cultural adjustment of current operations and/or programs.

➤ These donors rally others to the cause, they become philanthropists with NPO future opportunity interests and again, they will want to be included or partner.

The Grunge Philanthropist personality is a fun one. The grunge philanthropist is younger, and their personality originates from being layered in their philanthropic participation. The grunge philanthropist is committed to your cause or mission, but it is a very loose commitment. For example, these donors may give to your organization this year but next year they will give somewhere else.

Grunge philanthropists have a variety of nonprofits and crowd funding campaigns where they donate. If you would group all of them on a white board, chances are you will not be able to determine any pattern, passion, or relation to each of their donations and campaign involvement.

Grunge philanthropists are layered in their philanthropic participation and yearly activity. Some of the grunge philanthropists will see their giving as forwarding emails for a nonprofit. If they go downtown to an NPO and spend a day sorting at the warehouse, they may consider this activity (volunteering) as their giving. The Fundraiser needs to understand that a majority of these young grunge philanthropists are just beginning their philanthropic activity. Like anything else, the young in our culture want to be societal contrarians and this relates to their philanthropy too. Don't make the mistake of placing them in any of the outdated traditional philanthropic personalities – you will miss cultivating them completely.

Grunge philanthropists are enamored with the venture philanthropist and the entrepreneur philanthropist, but they haven't made enough money to obtain this admiration in their young income career(s). They love social justice projects or giving to environmental causes or feeding and clothing or providing water and wells. These campaigns are affordable, obtainable, and satisfying to them. They love giving to clothing stores that repurpose clothing like consignment shops. They believe they are cutting edge, but they are really mimicking some of the old guard Baby Boomers – the offspring coming out of the Great Depression. They love Go Fund Me and crowdfunding. They live on smartphone platforms such as Tik Tok, Instagram, and Twitter (Facebook is passé) where they can find immediate causes for the environment, animals, people who have had their homes burned down, health issues, or some personal crisis. They love that they can jump in and give something, then jump back out. The frenetic type of fundraising entices these grunge entrepreneurs. Giving $25 or $50 two, or three, times a month via a digital campaign is their passion.

Why do I call them grunge? The word "grunge" came from punk rock and hard rock music which was a combination of both. When the word began to be used on the billboard music charts, they would say the music is not punk or classic rock or even hard rock but elements of all three. These grunge philanthropists do not represent any of the seven traditional personalities. They are a mash-up of lower-level philanthropic participation without any consistent trends of distinct intentionality – in many ways, it is peer pressure and demographic populism that draw them into their philanthropy.

Grunge philanthropists give because it is emotional, and their giving can change – frenetically! One day they feel strongly about the social justice issue of race in America and their involvement is for thirty days. After these thirty days, they give to build water wells in South Africa.

As Fundraisers, we find many of these grunge philanthropist's graduating from our university and they are the donor who is the most challenging to cultivate, to understand, and to connect with alma mater giving. At CCU, we are constantly reviewing our contact reports and trying to understand what is it that they really want to do with their giving. In most of my meetings, we conclude you will only know them for thirty days then you will have to meet them again because they will change. As a donor centric Fundraiser, we've learned the necessity of staying in regular communication with our donors – this is also accurate for these young grunge donors. You will need to listen to them often to discover their passion and understand that it will change after a limited period of time.

From my experience, the grunge donor is a new personality and as a result, there is much to learn about it in the days ahead. Their demographic is mid-to-late twenties up to early thirties. I believe the grunge donor will mature when they marry, increase in income, purchase property, and welcome children to their family and their marriage. They may also need a few episodes of failure, heartache, and disappointment to draw them out of their youthfulness and into cultural needs, pain, and injustice(s). These maturing elements may also reduce the frenetic activity and help them define the scope of their philanthropic giving, its passion, and its desired outcome.

As I tell my team on a regular basis, these grunge donors need encouragement. As a Fundraiser, you cannot get discouraged with grunge characteristics and frenetic changes because, at the end of the day, they are apprentice philanthropists. They are engaged, involved, and willing to be generous. As a Fundraiser, we need to stay connected to them because three years down the road, we want to be their donor advisor for the three or four outcomes and impact missions they have selected.

Let me give you an example of two distinct grunge philanthropist (GP) characteristics.

The Crowdfunder is a "one and done, onto another" personality. The GP gives to be added to the giving numbers and to be seen as in membership with the cause they are supporting. She wants to see her donation in association with others to help reduce the expressed goal and the funds needed to make the campaign active. This GP will give once, maybe twice, to this campaign and then stop. They will check back to see how the campaign is moving. Once the campaign hits its goal, the GP is satisfied and will move on to look for another, similar Crowdfunding campaign.

Some of the Crowdfunders are **The Informal Donors**. The informal grunge philanthropists are "quiet, unannounced, and stealth." These youthful donors are old souls embedded in an innovative philanthropic culture. The informal grunge donors shop for mission-fit, or emotion-fit, opportunities. They do not want to be counted as an NPO's donor base giving partner. They don't want to be called upon or visited – even placed on an email communication release each month (they will unsubscribe). Like other donors, they will seek impact, outcomes, cultural social justice issues, and NPOs committed to not only immediate helps, but ultimate solutions!

Grunge Philanthropic Characteristics:

> ➤ They will not attend an event as a prospect donor.
> ➤ They will not reply to a mailed appeal letter, or survey.
> ➤ They will reluctantly offer their contact data, usually only name and cell number (text). They don't read printed mail.
> ➤ They will watch your NPO, call on occasion and ask a few questions, or inquire.
> ➤ Shockingly, they may ask that you do not send them any gift receipts. A number of young donors don't want gift receipts. They do their taxes but don't count their donations.
> ➤ They love the anonymity of their philanthropy and fear any/all recognition; this is why I call them an "old soul."
> ➤ They can feature many causes, many methods, and many digital innovations toward giving. The social media

influencers that I have encountered will make donations, give product(s), clothes, and food, to the Goodwill, will seek neighborhood needs and provide gift baskets, will orchestrate a "give ad you follow me" campaign, and even orchestrate other influencers to rally and collectively be philanthropic.

- ➤ They are presently wealthy, but unsure about its sustainability – so they give to help with their current windfall and dream about future greater opportunities.
- ➤ They have some life experience that enfolds into their platforms, media content, and their outcome-based philanthropy.
- ➤ They are active, frenetic, innovative, willing participants, and looking for larger impact through a larger audience.

Doing good is personal, professional, and very strategic – and the best part, their philanthropical impacts are still being honed and maturing.

The Blended and Ingenious

Let me highlight further a story of an isolated, business-model example of a blended effort between the venture and entrepreneur philanthropist mindset – even a grunge philanthropist.

Today's donors are, themselves, ingenious in their fundraising ideas and innovation. Many of today's donors are ingenious in their philanthropic passions. The blended venture-entrepreneur donor characteristics are more and more evident in performing arts and media productions.

No table of contents entries found. During my tenure at CCU I have been blessed to know Jerry B. Jenkins, a university Board member, a very generous donor, and a dear friend. Jerry's son is Dallas Jenkins, a recent innovative filmmaker sensation. Millions of viewers have downloaded Dallas' smart phone app entitled "The Chosen." The app features a series saga about the life and times of Jesus Christ and his disciples. Dallas is the creative genius behind the production's success, displaying the "chip off the old block" cultural and professional success of his father, Jerry's, the co-author of the *Left Behind* series of novels. The Jenkins senior's books sold tens of millions of copies and topped national bestseller lists in the 1990's.

Dallas is mimicking his father's cultural success via digital technology, the world of on-demand viewership, and a disruptive concept of blending investors, philanthropists, and an army of devout supports.

The genius behind Dallas' work with "The Chosen" is his business model. It features a strict and defined philanthropic platform that can be combined with an investors' opportunity. Dallas' goal was to mix altruism and evangelism, urging *The Chosen* fans to chip in money to keep a drama about Jesus and his teaching free for anyone to watch.

As *Wall Street Journal* writer John Jurgensen writes, "The show grew out of a short film and fundraising messages Mr. Jenkins posted online in 2017. Some 16,000 people paid at least $100 each to fund the shooting of the first season in 2018, budgeted at $11 million. In exchange, this flock of financial backers got an equity stake in the company that produced the show. They received shares in The

Chosen LLC through an offering process filed with the Securities and Exchange Commission."[12]

This venture-entrepreneur characteristic has birthed one of the most ingenious business models I have ever experienced. *The Chosen* has super-charged the crowd funding model to sustain production through multiple seasons. *The Chosen* is free to watch, and viewers have poured over $40 million (and counting) into the production budget – enough to pay for three of the seven seasons planned in the series. At present 16 episodes have been viewed 312 million times. *The Chosen's* crowd fundraising has eclipsed $6 million via Kickstarter as Season 3 was released in March of 2022.

The blended funding mixture of investors, altruism, and the devout (traditional personalities) and the venture, entrepreneur, and grunge characteristics has kept the production free to anyone who desires to download the app and watch. It has also provided investment revenue for start-up costs and future production set designs and business ventures and satisfied the devout a professional – competitive Hollywood-quality evangelical outcomes.

I share this amazing story to remind and *encourage* you that a donor-centric philosophy must feature an open-mindedness to new ideas, philanthropic innovations, and cutting-edge implementation. My fellow Fundraiser, what was, is no longer. The old-school, traditional philanthropy and philanthropists still exist, but they are represented by a growing minority in the philanthropic population. Fundraising futures rest in an intentional relational dance between the missional ideations of today's NPOs and the innovative characteristic

---

[12] *Crowdfunding the New Testament*, WSJ, November 27, 2021.

of the venture and entrepreneur donors. Let me encourage you to embrace the change, prepare for this change, and operate your philanthropical systems in anticipation for this change.

The Donor's Person over the Pocket

You can look at a donor's pocket all day long and make an ask and hope they will give (usually a one-time shot).

Don't look at the pocket.

Look directly at the person.

When you build a relationship with the person (donor), you will understand the donor's heart, thus the donor's pocket. As a donor advisor, I want to understand this person so I can advise them how best to be philanthropic for their impact and outcome.

It used to be you would meet donors and show them all the different ways they could give at different levels and meet the needs of the nonprofit organization. This method was a constant barrier, and I encourage my team and colleagues to refuse to use this method any longer. You meet the donor, learn who they are, listen twice as much you talk, you journal, and contact report the experience, and you get to know their personality. As I understand the donor and their distinct personality, I can be a donor advisor, earn their valued trust and help them accomplish their ultimate goals through their distinct philanthropy.

Chapter Five

Healthy Portfolio Management

"When we change our mindset from asking people for money to developing relationships that allow people to give, we allow them to match their passions and dreams to the people we serve; it changes the entire approach."[13] Joseph Tumolo, *"Go See People and Grow Your Fundraising"*

On the surface, portfolio work might not seem like a critical issue for Fundraisers. I was having lunch with Scott Lumpkin, a reputable Denver philanthropic consultant. Both of us know and work with a number of philanthropic Major Gift Officers. A frequent weakness, and even apathy, is fine tuning your skills in managing a donor-centric portfolio. Scott said, "The most prevalent area of weakness for local nonprofit organizations is their lack of understanding of how to manage their donor portfolios. It's the single greatest detriment to fundraising success and sustainability."

For fundraising success or failure, portfolio management success is a major factor. When nonprofit organizations are asked about the

---

[13] Joseph Tumolo, *Go See People Grow Your Fundraising Program* (SkillBites Publishing, 2017), 67-69.

state of their portfolios, a majority of directors and executives claim they operate a healthy and active portfolio process. But when you take a closer look, the evidence proves they do not have a winning portfolio process, and the lack of this process is hurting philanthropic futures and mission outcomes across the fundraising landscape. Professional Fundraisers must learn how to manage their portfolios properly. In fact, portfolio management is dependent on strategic intention and ongoing Fundraiser attention. Much of this process failure springs from a lack of understanding. You can do portfolio management wrong and, in many ways, if you do it wrong, it is worse than doing nothing at all. Major Gift Officers contend they are communicating with their portfolio donors, but communication isn't enough. Success comes from connecting, building trust, and moving the relationship into a professional role of philanthropic advising. The real bullseye is to manage these portfolios professionally, with excellence, and in great priority for the success of the donor and the nonprofit.

Many nonprofits will say they have healthy and active donor portfolios but when you take a closer look, they do not. In the introduction, I talked about Sarah who contended she had 680 donors in her portfolio, which is simply impossible. This is actually worse than no portfolio management because it is impossible to manage 680 donors in one MGO's portfolio.

The best way I know how to explain the importance of portfolio management is to compare it to financial wealth management. Many major donors have a personal financial, or wealth manager. My long-time personal wealth manager is Doug McFarlane. From my experience with financial managers, Doug is one of the best. When I hear people describe the characteristics of a professional portfolio manager, I immediately think of Doug and his tremendous skill set.

What Is a Donor Portfolio?

Let's go back to the story of Sarah, the donor hoarder. As mentioned, she had those 680 donors in her donor adviser portfolio. To Sarah's credit, she at least had a portfolio. The biggest weakness in any nonprofit organization is the lack of assigning and correctly managing **a healthy donor portfolio**. A healthy portfolio has:

- Between 75-100 active donors with an expressed mission affinity (no more).

- An assigned community of constituents that a professional "Donor Advisor" (not a myopic Fundraiser) manages.

- Intentionally immersed into purpose-driven philanthropic conversations.

- Implementing the "donor-centric cultivation cycle" (Ch. 3) for any necessary and assigned new donors or prospective donors.

- Frequent communications through channels and the donor determines the frequency.

- A laser beam focus on building trust, authenticity, and a mature professional relationship.

James M. Langley in *The Future of Fundraising* brings clarity on this distinction. James has classified the donor adviser versus the Fundraiser in activities labeled as *Hunters* versus *Growers*:[14]

---

[14] James M. Langley, *The Future of Fundraising* (Academic Impressions,

> *Hunters* believe, "The more we get out 'into the field' or commit ourselves to being 'road warriors,' and the more we ask, the better our chances of meeting or exceeding our annuals goals."
>
> *Growers* believe, "The more we nurture the good in people by listening respectfully to them, aligning our interests with them, and delivering on our promises to them, the more bountiful our shared harvest will be over time."

Major Gift Officers need to look at their portfolios from a grower perspective instead of a hunter perspective.

In 2003, I met Doug McFarland when our family moved across the street from his family when living in California. Our families were neighbors for over fifteen years, until 2018 when we relocated to Colorado. Doug and his wife know my family, my kids, and our grandkids. During my tenure as vice president at William Jessup University, Doug got involved with my missional passions for Christ-centered higher education and became an individual donor to support me, the university, and to learn more about my job.

For me, Doug manages a diversified fund that I invest through Robert W. Baird Financial, his professional firm. I'm in Doug's portfolio of clients. Professionally, I have patterned a lot of my portfolio management for donors by watching and learning from Doug. He has earned a Five Star Wealth Manager Award from *Sacramento Magazine* which he has received for 11 consecutive

Denver, CO., 2020), 51-55.

years. Wealth managers receive this award from their peers and firms based on ten objective criteria such as client retention rates, client assets administered, and a favorable regulatory history. The key characteristics are integrity, honesty, and ethics. These managers focus on improving the lives of their clients and their families as they provide attentive financial services and customer care. Doug's commitment to a client-first philosophy, collegial teamwork and personal service has earned him this best-in-class recognition.

As a wealth manager, Doug has introduced me to prospective donors for the benefit of William Jessup University's mission. Doug has also introduced me to countless people through email or an informal coffee meeting at his office in Roseville, California. Also, he has included me in corporate events and gatherings so people could meet me and I would have the opportunity to meet them. He's not just concerned with my finances, but Doug is also concerned with me and my professional success and well-being as an industry leader.

This is the same way a Major Gift Officer needs to operate with a donor in their portfolio management. Doug has also supported my work at Colorado Christian University and even asked his high school daughter to consider visiting CCU to "check things out and share a lunch with Mr. and Mrs. Hogue."

While Doug is a trusted family friend and former neighbor, he also knows how to divide his professional portfolio role against his personal family connections. He is a master in portfolio cultivation, authenticity, and personal investor-centric interests. When we speak together, he listens, frequently connects me with investment opportunities, and is constantly touching base to see how I am doing in life, professionally, and with my investments. Truth here – when I want to improve my efforts and management of my portfolio of donors, I think of my good friend and brother Doug.

In the introduction, I included a number of stories about Major Gift Officers who believed they were doing portfolio management with their donors. My experience and research show on average, a frustrated Major Gift Officer stays in their role for 12 to 18 months, then they leave the position because they cannot build success, and they find nothing but great frustration in attempting to cultivate a large portfolio. Their approach to strategic portfolio management is a "spray and pray" approach to connecting via a series of emails or mass letters. Poor portfolio management is the Achilles heel to Fundraising and leads to constant change with MGOs and donors as well.

While I was at William Jessup University, one day a leading, major donor named Jack called and said, "Eric, I've been giving to the university for fifteen years and my lead contact in your office has changed four times. How long are you going to be here, and can I call you directly? I want to be in touch with someone who understands what my wife and I want to do with our giving." I could hear the frustration in Jack's voice, so I added him to my donor portfolio and worked with Jack throughout my remaining six years at the university – the longest running MGO in his personal donor history to that point in time. Jack and his wife, to this date, are major donors for Jessup University and have been honored with their name attached to a basketball court in the new Warrior Arena in Rocklin, California.

As mentioned several times, a realistic donor portfolio is 75 to 100 donors where you are intentional on building a relationship, listening to the donor and advising them on the impact, outcomes, and intentionality of their philanthropy. Why 75 to 100 donors in a portfolio – why not 100-175? To answer this common request, let's think about our available time to work with our donors as it relates to life work balance. About a third of our days are weekends, vacation, and personal time with family. Another third is meetings, attending training, and filling out contact reports and other fundraising work. Then the final third involves these 75 to 100 donor relationships that you can successfully manage in a portfolio and in your work life.

Here's a dose of fundraising reality: How can relationships be built with major donors when MGOs don't stay long enough in the job? I have spoken to a number of CCU donors who informed me upon my arrival, "Eric, I hope you and your team stay in place for a few years. It is so frustrating for me and my wife when we have to start over with a new assigned advisor in your shop." As a Fundraiser, frustration is not our desired outcome for the donor nor the onset of the "frustrated Fundraiser."

I say it again – the greatest threat to achieving successful donor-centric philanthropy can be chalked up to poorly designed and managed donor portfolios. When you combine weak portfolio performance with the high turnover rates for Major Gift Officer that cause donors to constantly be re-introducing to your donor base, you begin to understand how it is a challenge for every nonprofit to become successful. I don't care what size shop or operation you represent as a Fundraiser; you must give the design and the appropriate activity to portfolio development priority.

If your employee retention and your donor retention are consistently low, your nonprofit organization will not experience sustainable philanthropic success. To build a strong portfolio management system, you will need to address two areas: (1) Create a system to support and train professional Major Gift Officers so they become trusted donor advisors, and (2) teach appropriate designs and processes for professional portfolio management.

How to Organize Your Portfolios

The majority of fundraising organizations use geography to assign and organize Major Gift Officers portfolios. For example, a certain MGO will be assigned to cover the southwest part of the United States while another MGO has the northeastern states, and another MGO will cover the Midwest region. Whenever I hear this portfolio management from an MGO, it screams of Fundraiser-centric philosophies. If an organization uses geography or location to assign portfolios, you will hear the Fundraiser say things like, "That's my region" or worse yet, "that's my turf."

The process of this geographic assignment focuses on the Major Gift Officer, the operational budget, and clear-cut geographical location. Nothing in this assignment decision represents the donor's distinctive personality and philanthropic characteristics. When the donors are divided according to geography, the process is more equitable and affordable operationally. But is that the goal? Should we be concerned about travel expenses? Or should we be concerned about the investment into real donor-centric relationships and their philanthropic longevity?

Instead of using geography to organize your portfolios, there is a better approach. I suggest you match your Major Gift Officers with donors who fit their personalities, interests, and philanthropic ideologies including their skillsets – even lifestyle demographics. In our portfolio meetings, we use a template discussion when we match donors with a Major Gift Officer. These are some of the areas of consideration:

- Is the donor close to considering a planned gift? If this donor is older, then assign a seasoned MGO who understands planned giving vehicles.
- Is the donor interested in athletics, academics, or adult learners who attend CCU online?
- Is the donor a widower, and would they appreciate (be more comfortable) with a male, or female Major Gift Officer?
- Is the donor interested in capital campaigns, or are they intentional about student scholarships, or faculty endowments?
- Is the donor an alum, a parent, or a former faculty member at a different school, or university?
- What is the age demographic of the donors? Does the donor still have children at home and would a Major Gift Officer with children at home be a better fit?

These filtering questions are some examples of what should be used with donor portfolio assignments helping the donor portfolio assignment to be more about donor-centric intentions versus simple geography. You take time to assign Major Gift Officer portfolios with intent that the donor-centric relationship involves similarities, closely aligned life experiences, and a commonality of intentional outcomes.

Here are a few general discovery distinctions of your donors to utilize in your portfolio assignments:

Philanthropy:

Planned Gifts

Scholarships

Capital Campaigns

Operations

Debt or Threat Relief

Endowments

Innovation

Demographics:

Age

Male, Female

Married

Widowed, Widower

Former Executive

Young Married

Personality:

Innovative

Venture

Entrepreneur

Grunge

Aggressive

Long-Term Planning

Annual Fund (Scholarships)

Student-Driven

Mission-Driven

In general, every Major Gift Officer should be able to handle diverse categories but some of your staff will be better in some areas than another. On my staff at CCU, Mark is my senior director of major giving and planned gifts. Under normal circumstances, I would not assign Mark to a donor who wants to give to the unrestricted giving, or an NPO's operational budget, because it is not a good fit for Mark. He is better fit for someone who is in the category of planned gifts or capital campaigns. As a result, Mark will get more donors in that particular genre of philanthropy than donors who are thinking about scholarships or debt relief.

In our shop, we meet periodically and discuss our assigned portfolios. A report is generated featuring all of our qualifying first-time donors. Someone on our team does prospect research on these donors to see about their giving pattern, their interests, and other philanthropic information to see if the donors have given to other universities or other similar organizations. We can determine their basic demographics and wealth screening to know their income on a gross annual basis. During our collegial portfolio meeting, we look at each one and ask, "Does this donor need to be in a portfolio, or should we allow them to give organically?" If we decide they don't go in a portfolio, then we communicate with them in a different way than assigning it to a Major Gift Officer. If we think this donor is a prospect that we could move into a more intentional giving portfolio and support of the university, then they go into an assigned and specific portfolio. The portfolio meeting is vital – for the MGO and the donors. Discussing donor activities and interest is good for the NPO and it is good for the donor and their relationship with their assigned donor advisors.

For the majority of these new donors, they are not assigned to a portfolio. To get assigned they have to, what we call, "wave a flag" or show they have an immediate intention to do something ongoing or intentional to support the nonprofit organization. If they do not immediately enter a portfolio, we actively connect to the non-profit's activities and mission in various ways. The donor's involvement, questions, and interest in these activities help us determine their passions and desired philanthropic role for the mission. For every ten donors that we consider, about 1.5 are assigned to a portfolio. Some weeks it is two donors and other weeks it is only one. If they are not assigned, then they will be contacted through our annual fund officers or receive simple communications from the office to allow them to connect in areas that pique their interest and desired philanthropic passions. If they are alumni of the university, then our alumni director will connect with them personally.

Once a year at CCU, we have a Giving Day online where the money goes to student scholarships and campus projects. We might have a donor give $100 to this campaign. When they do we employ some intentional research on this donor, to learn more about them and their philanthropic interests. We might discover the donor and his wife are recent CCU graduates and four years into employment with their new jobs. We assume they still have some student debt and greatly appreciate that they gave $100, but we're not going to cultivate them in a major gift portfolio. They are appreciative of their alma mater, and they're just starting out in their married and professional lives together . . . and in their philanthropic life. Instead, we assign these wonderful alumni donors to our annual fund director so he, and his staff, can communicate with them on a regular basis and discover where, when, and how they might desire to participate in the future.

The donors who end up in a portfolio with a Major Gift Officer are highly intentional people with great philanthropic means and intentionality. These donors are asking for someone from the NPO to advise them and build a relationship with them in order to achieve the greatest impact with their giving and their generous philanthropy.

As we sit together around a conference table, we'll match the donors with the expertise of the various Major Gift Officers. We take the time to have those conversations and make sure the donor is going to fit with the right person. Sometimes we discuss someone who isn't really a fit to be in a portfolio and we move them out into another process. The management of portfolios is not always cut and dried. It can be very fluid and flexible.

In contrast to the way I've described our meetings, I have sat through portfolio meetings where Major Gift Officers discuss new donors and explain that they are in their portfolio because of geography. These words about donors feel "sales-ish" where a Fundraiser is staking out his territory and looks at donors as property. This Fundraiser is covering an assigned geography that simply needs to be fertilized, watered, plowed, and harvested during the solicitation season. When I hear such conversations, I don't like it. If I can sense it then the donor can sense it, and the resulting relationship becomes transactional. These types of assignments are not donor-centric but Fundraiser-centric and need to be redesigned.

In contrast, I love when portfolios are assigned because of relationships and distinct characteristics. There is nothing better than telling a donor, "I'm flying to see you."

They may ask, "There isn't another donor or partner you're coming to see?"

The major gift officer says, "No, I'm getting on a plane to meet with you personally." I have had a couple of donors confirm that they were donating, or making a pledge, and keep track of the number of visits I scheduled with them.

At the close of our time they offer, "Here is a check for your many flights and meals meeting with me to determine this donation." Honesty is what donors want from their donor advisor. They desire integrity, transparency, and they want to learn from their donor advisor, as well as have them operate as respectful listeners. Donors want their motivations to be understood. They want authentic, accountable advisors of philanthropy to represent them and not sales individuals who serve their territory. The Fundraiser demonstrates patient relationships, follow through and the impact upon the organization from the donor's generosity and donations. The Major Gift Officer needs to see her portfolio as nurtured professional relationships of impact, not wealthy territorial donors to help meet projected fundraising goals. Assigning portfolios geographically is a lazy practice which is filled with Major Gift Officer frustrations and donor advisor changes. If you want donor retention and longevity from your Major Gift Officers, then put relatable intentional people together. With this donor-centric management style, you will be able to watch the growth in trust, communication, and professionalism. The process requires time and energy to connect portfolios to real donor advising relationships and advisement for you to deliver success for the donor, the Major Gift Officer and the nonprofit's impact and mission outcomes.

Recognition and Reward (the "TED Talk" on paying well)

If you are going to put this much effort into your Major Gift Officers and the management of donor portfolios, then you need to be intentional about how you pay your donor-facing professionals. In a donor-centric and portfolio-focused philanthropic strategy, we are handing prized donors over to Major Gift Officers who nurture these relationships to enjoy great longevity. From my experience, a wide majority of nonprofits always want to limit what they pay their MGOs. I wholeheartedly disagree with these income limitations. Instead, I believe professional trained and experienced MGOs should be paid what they are worth to the NPO and to the donors.

Fundraising is a resource center for charity operations. The rule of thumb in business is to fund your resource centers so they can drive success, versus limiting them in personal growth.

To back up this distinct view, I point to a controversial TED Talk featuring Dan Pallotta, a cultural activist and professional Fundraiser. Dan's presentation entitled *"The Way We Think About Charity is Dead Wrong"* is still available to review via YouTube by searching the title via TED Talks lecturers. Dan's 15-minute presentation called out the double standard that drives our broken relationship to charities and donors as compared to the private sector and business. Here was the crux of Dan's argument: "Too many nonprofit organizations are praised and celebrated for how little they spend on innovative operations and professional salaries, versus what they get done, achieve, and remedy through their mission(s)."[15]

In the private sector, if Microsoft hires four vice presidents and those VPs go out and create an increasing margin of income over five years, no one complains when they get a 150% increase on their salary because they are turning a profit for the company. The respectful and appreciative conversation surrounding earned, merited, and increased wages is a welcomed topic for private businesses and the general marketplace. But when this topic is applied to nonprofits, charities, or ministries, it immediately becomes taboo – even ethically unacceptable to discuss or consider. In the church setting, we love our pastor, and our church is growing, but in general we don't reward him for that growth. We seem to have a theological or exegetical

---

[15] Dan Pallotta, *The Way We Think About Charity is Dead Wrong*, YouTube, TED Talk, February 2013.

application that believes we need to keep him lean and hungry so we maintain his (impoverished) salary so he isn't paid too much and can relate to the common, lower income demographic(s) church member. Don't scoff at this implied reasoning – I have heard it, experienced it, and know it is a templated evaluation for directors, pastors, and executives of nonprofits, ministries, and charities.

If you have a Major Gift Officer who is cultivating 75 to 100 donors and doing it in a respectful donor-centric, professional manner, and that portfolio is increasing year after year in gifts to the University, then you had better pay that gift officer well as a reward and incentive for a job well done. Believe me, if you don't, someone eventually will. It is wholly hypocritical for Board and Trustees to represent this in their personal private sector operations only to deny this human reality in the nonprofit sector they serve.

Dan is highlighting a reality. In the private sector, salaries are tied to success and gained profit margins. In nonprofits, salaries are usually static, remedial, and based on equal comparisons with similar (other) nonprofits. For nonprofits, a base salary usually only increases through the annual cost of living adjustment (COLA) – and that variable is debated over and over before its activation.

Pallotta's argument is clear and absolute. He believes nonprofits need to dream big, solve big problems, and reward success like the private sector even if it comes with increased expenses, operations, and salary costs. In his 15-minute TED Talk which has been viewed over five million times, Pallotta argues we need to shift how we think about changing the world through nonprofits with their distinct and compelling mission(s).

Remember this truth: **the prohibition of failure kills innovation**. Pallotta's argument goes to the heart of tying a gift officer's pay to the operational innovations and determined successes a nonprofit designs and desires to invest. This limiting factor on nonprofits, operational budgets and successful employees' salaries is hypocritical and mission prohibitive. We can watch a multi-million-dollar private sector company risk millions on a new line of technical entertainment, digital applications, or diversifying products, and if (when) the effort falls flat and millions are lost, the response is "great idea, great effort, give it another shot."

But when a nonprofit attempts to make a large investment through innovation, aggressive market strategies, or hiring the brightest and the best talent to operate their fundraising shop, the objections are heard of "cost per dollar raised," or "you didn't return at least a 4-to-1 on expenses," or you're not at our threshold of 75% toward cost to build." To me, such objections are self-limiting to the mission and success your NPO states to be mission critical. If you see operational budgets as investments toward bigger and better success in the private sector, why does the nonprofit constantly label operational budgets and employee salaries as a drag on the bottom line and a fiscal expense?

If you have a good MGO who manages their portfolio professionally and successfully, why is it necessary to compare their salary to other similar positions at schools, ministries, and nonprofits? Are those MGOs as good as your prized overachiever? Isn't that a decision you should be making internally? No one ever said, "Tom Brady is the greatest quarterback in NFL history and his performance is second to none. Let's do a salary comparison with the other NFL quarterbacks to determine his egalitarian salary target." If New England, or Tampa Bay had engineered this practice with Brady, Tom's talent and abilities would have played out in another NFL market and Tampa Bay would have never acquired him for a chance at a Super Bowl championship.

This comparison to a quarterback goes for successful major gift performers and their donor-centric skills. If your lead MGO's are not well compensated and you constantly need to hire new, more affordable major gift officers, this repetitive outcome will directly affect the success of your organization's mission and your fundraising success. Your nonprofit will be left with an egalitarian compensation package married to a limited professional, tenured, and static operation. Your future will be hindered by retention issues – both internally and externally with your lead donors.

From my experience in this area, if you assign a major gift officer 75 to 100 donors in a portfolio, an effective donor-centric MGO will produce a 3-to-1 return on their salary after 18 months in the position. That ratio will double in 1.5 years as your professional MGO works with his or her donors to achieve a successful donor advisement. Let me explain it in a different format: If you hire a major gift officer at a salary rate of $100,000 annually, in 18 months, this individual should be actively cultivating donations projected to $300,000. In 1.5 years, or donor cultivation activity within three fiscal campaigns, this major gift officer should be projecting over $600,000, and headed toward the $1 million mark in donations and planned gifts from their portfolio partners. As success develops over the next two to three years, you will be forced to adjust their salary to retain, reward, and incentivize them – and this needs to be above and beyond an annual cost of living increase (COLA). When successful, mission-fit Major Gift Officers are compensated in this fashion, they produce another "value asset" for the nonprofit's philanthropy which is **donor retention**. The longer the major gift officer remains happily in the position, building a trusted donor advisor role with his or her portfolio members, the more retention and increased philanthropy these valuable nonprofit representatives will produce.

I have yet to run across a donor who scolded me or my NPO for giving lead MGOs a merited increase in pay. "Eric, I love Brent." Brent is the donor advisor that has been assigned through the university. "Brent is great, and he really listens to us. He has applied our donations and replied to us about the impact and outcome. He has been professional and operated with integrity and represents your university and Christ centered mission perfectly."

"I'm glad to hear this feedback. We just gave Brent a raise," I may respond. I have never had a donor respond with, "Well, why did you do that?" Instead, whenever I say something about our system of rewarding Brent, donors always endorse, "Well, you better take care of Brent because I want you to keep him around. He is the best representative of our giving to your NPO we have ever experienced." If the donors are thinking in this way, why aren't we? Good people doing good work are valuable to the nonprofit organization and ultimate producers of higher donor retention rates that lead to quality NPO sustainable futures.

I frequently find myself in a situation where my budget manager(s) want me to pay a major gift officer through metrics driven by comparison salary scales. I respectfully respond, "I don't care about the comparative salaries. I care about how this major gift officer is taking care of our donors and the amount of donations she is overseeing in a donor-centric fashion. The donors are happy. The MGO is happy, and I am happy, and our donations are increasing which is all I care about. I want to keep her around for a long time. Let's not be short-sighted on this budget decision." In a real-world economy, our salaries are not equal, our roles are not equal, and the systems we work within (for) are not equal. Pay scale is a strategy that leads to profitability. I have heard many successful CEO's comment, "For years I focused on profits, then I decided to focus on people – the moment I made this switch my company gained profitability."

I know this is controversial. I completely understand that this compensation ideology is different than the typical nonprofit ideology. The "bean counters" believe every major gift officer should be paid equally. They will research what other organizations are paying their MGOs to prove their point and solidify an argument. Respectfully, I don't want to ask other universities what my major gift officers are worth in my specific operation. I know what they are worth. If my shop is not doing their job, then I will face the heat. But if my department and shop is doing their job, I will make my decision about compensation independent of what other universities are doing in the area of compensation. There is nothing wrong in paying good people for good work and success. A well-trained and supported

MGO will work and thrive in structured, frequent personal development through one-on-one coaching, seminar attendance, and specific continuing education. Taking these actions will move you, your MGO, your mission, and your donors to the 'next level' faster and with more measurable sustainability.

Needed Skills for a Major Gift Officer

I am frequently asked about the necessary skill-sets needed to be a successful donor-centric major gift officer (MGO). Here are two MGO skills, or lenses, that need to be consistently sharpened for the successful MGO toolbox.

Excellent Writing Ability

There is a common misconception in the Fundraising community that a Major Gift Officer has to be an extroverted personality and to be good at talking. From my experience, this is not accurate. A better, more critical skill is to be an excellent communicator or writer. As an MGO with a donor portfolio, you are going to be writing many letters, emails, texts, and thank you cards. In addition, you are going to write many proposals for donors to consider. Depending upon your job description, you may also be asked to write strategic and systematic fundraising appeal letters – this is especially true at a university or any type of higher education.

Let me start this section off with a bit of a higher education rant. There has been a great loss of appreciation for a quality liberal arts education in America. The liberal arts are the traditional academic programs in Western higher education. The liberal arts are best understood as a learned skill rather than the niche or specific skills of the fine arts. The study here is more general and is in preparation for each graduate to study toward future success in a vocation or profession. In these general studies the student learns how to think critically, speak or communicate broadly, read comprehensively, and write proficiently.

For the MGO, all of these skills are important, but none more so than the ability to communicate, especially writing proficiency. For major gift officers, the ability to write professional letters, comprehensive reports, donor-centric proposals, thank you letters, and an occasional newsletter is the "spade work" of tending your portfolio. As an MGO, if you do not have the confidence to write well, speak well, and communicate maturely, you need to learn to do so to be successful.

When I interview a prospective MGO, I ask them to write a letter to a donor. When I read what they have written, I'm surprised. The reality of the necessity of this communication skill hits me personally. I was not a great writer growing up, and I continue to rest heavily upon quality editing. I was much worse in the earlier years of my broadcast career. The lack of a good writing acumen and skill set caused great personal pain and tremendous barriers in my twenties and early thirties.

I had to work at being a better writer – and I had to work hard! I discovered the importance of writing as a sophomore in high school. My English teacher, Polly Haden Doyle, first grabbed my attention in a Literature class, gently highlighting that I needed some basic mastery skills of English rules and writing. Ms. Haden noticed my extroverted personality, which was dependent upon my verbal skills versus my writing skills. She decided to intervene and bring it to my attention in high school.

After a class writing assignment, she approached me. "Eric, I need to ask you about your paper." She handed me the red inked notebook paper bound in a paper binder. "I am sorry, but I cannot give you more than a C- on your work. You had so much to say in your story, but I could not get past all of your spelling, grammar, tense, and fragmented sentence structure to enjoy it."

I sheepishly responded, "Ms. Haden, I'm just not a good writer."

She quickly replied, "This is why you're in my class. We are going to change this weakness. You can do so much better than C-level work. I have an idea."

Feeling a bit fearful and curious, I said, "What is it?"

"I want you to join the high school newspaper staff. You can write about topics where you have passion and interest. As you write, I'll help you edit, teach you better rules and give you tools for writing. You will face what every writer fears — which is your peers reading your work."

My skills didn't change overnight. I continued to fear editing, reviews, and peer readership. My two-year stint on the staff of the Louisville Senior High School *Spotlight* marked my first step toward a sincere effort to address my writing skills.

During my thirty-plus year radio career, my willingness to put myself out there through public speaking, critical thinking, mass communicating, and writing presented itself in a daily radio blog web page which garnered thousands of readers in Northern California.

After a few years of being called out on my bad grammar, spelling, and sentence structures, I was forced – by continual embarrassment – to improve. Eventually an editor at the *Sacramento Bee* occasionally asked me to write political and cultural opinion editorials on a periodic schedule. With each step my skills improved.

Any MGO who wants to connect with his or her portfolio must have skills to speak, think, communicate, and write well. If you can't communicate through the written word, you will drive your donors crazy making (too) frequent telephone calls. I encourage you to practice your writing skills and continue to master this important skill and begin today.

Money Ideology

How a major gift officer views money is a big issue as you design and assign portfolios. Joseph Tumolo (*Go See People,* Skill bites Publishing) writes, "People become uncomfortable when the topic of money arises because it is very personal and makes us feel vulnerable. Our money stories are often formed at an early age by watching those around us."[16]

Joseph is absolutely right. Our childhood can be a hotbed of illicit money perspectives. My father lost his job when I was in high school. Money became a rare commodity when I began to leave home and launch out on my own. My view of money and those people who had a lot of it were challenged during my early college years and into my early media career.

---

[16] Joseph Tumolo, *Go See People Grow Your Fundraising Program* (SkillBites Publishing, 2017), 23-27.

There are various clichés about money, many negative, such as, "Money doesn't grow on trees." Or the advice that, "It's not polite to talk to people about money." Or there are heavily negative comments like, "The rich just keep on getting richer." Everyone raised in the church has heard that, "the love of money is evil." I know a number of pastors, close personal friends of mine, who will not preach on money because it is uncomfortable for them or for their congregation.

If an MGO maintains a bad perspective or unhealthy ideology toward money, it can erode his/her confidence to discuss money and its value, importance, and ability. A tainted bias of wealthy people can lead you to become judgmental, disrespectful, envious and, at times subjectively, to covet wealth. There has to be a maturity and understanding about money which goes back to Doug McFarland, my wealth manager. If you are going to sit in front of wealthy individuals, you need the right perspective about the utility of money. You have to understand that God prescribed wealth through hard work, and today's donors are giving from a generous heart for the good of mankind. Major Gift Officers must learn to gather this money in a mature and professional manner. If a Fundraiser has any hidden negative perspectives about money, it will eventually come out before the donor or others.

During my second year at William Jessup University, Nancy, a major gift officer, returned to the office after meeting one of her donors in the Bay Area. During the meeting, Nancy offered an acutely prepared proposal to Jerome and Harriet. "This proposal isn't enough," Jerome said. "We want to give more over a longer period of time. We'd like you to consider not just our first gift but also a second and third gift to this academic program." Nancy did a professional job of cultivating and presenting this proposal to the right donor and with the right donor-centric process.

When Nancy came into my office to discuss her meeting and how to expand her proposal, she said, "Eric, have you ever sat in front of a donor, and they are just filthy rich? Jerome and Harriet don't even know it. I was amazed how quickly they went from phase one to phase three and didn't even think about it. Can you image what their life is like and how easy it must be for them?"

It was an unguarded moment for Nancy, to say the least.

We had a lengthy conversation about her comments. I asked, "Can you work with these donors going forward or is the tainted ideology going to become a barrier?" We worked on it for a month and a half. Nancy narrowed her attitude to her childhood when her dad lost his job and that she had to go to work early in her life. Because Nancy had to work, she was unable to be a cheerleader and carried some bitterness about that season in her life. To her credit, Nancy met with her pastor and talked through this situation. She worked on her judgmental ideology and became successful as a major gift officer.

In a similar pattern, my early executive assistant at CCU, Lois, walked into my office one afternoon with the mail and gave me a few envelopes featuring donations. She waited for me to open the envelopes, stood gazing at the checks, and on numerous occasions she commented, "It must be nice to have so much money that you can give away a million dollars." Eventually, Lois was transitioned from her role as my EA when she stated to a coworker in the office, "These donors have so much money. Why don't they just give me a check?"

Her flippant expression, constant money-worship, and personalization of the comments eventually cost Lois her job. This type of perspective, commentary, and overt covetousness cannot go unaddressed – or allowed to take root in a donor-centric fundraising department.

I meet with every new MGO and take them through a self-analysis of their money ideology. While Human Resources researches each of my staff members according to credit problems, bankruptcies, and debt loads, I add a few weeks of money ideology training. The goal is to find a positive money ideology, versus a negative or envious one. Money can bring numerous personalities, human characteristics, and bent perspectives to the surface in a hurry. It is best to locate and weed out these undesirable attitudes from your staff as fast as possible.

Make A Difference in the World

The heart of the donor intends to make a difference in the world. The Apostle Paul referenced this in his letter to the church at Corinth. In essence, in 2 Corinthians chapter 8, Paul is commenting on how the act of giving is less important than the heart behind it.

Paul believed the donor's willingness to give is a vital part of the Christian's discipleship. The gifts amount to a tangible expression of their love for others, for truth, and for remedy of a painful, fallen world. These early donors understood the ramifications of the work that needed to be done to proclaim the cause of Christ, the mission of the gospel.

In this chapter, Paul sets out to explain why the philanthropy needed for the Christians in Jerusalem would be beneficial. The chief problem with the donors of Corinth was not their lack of support due to unwillingness, but they lacked follow through. In their hearts, they had committed to providing the necessary financial assistance but were not following through on their promise.

Apparently, the Corinthian donors had begun a collection or a cultivated pledge drive for a need of Jerusalem's Christian church. But their efforts waned and fell off. Paul was referencing the necessity to keep one's commitments to do good. In Ecclesiastes 5, the author states, "It is better that you should not vow than that you should vow and not pay (donate)." As a portfolio manager, Paul reminded the donors of their intentions and offered an intentional conversation about the cause and outcome(s).

If I can stretch a bit as an exegete, as well as bending of my direct application of this Scriptural reference, the Apostle Paul operated as a Major Gift Officer. He was not asking the Corinthian donors to give what they did not have or to, "sacrifice so much that it hurts." He was only asking that they be willing to give and to fulfill their pledge(s). The size of the gift mattered less than the act of giving and its motivation. Paul knew the Corinthian donors' passions, intentionality, and desired impact. He knew they wanted to give and that their gifts were good, vital, and full of outcomes that satisfy the donor(s).

Paul was also performing as a donor advisor. He knew the Corinthians' hearts and passions. He had a relationship with them. He was communicating with them, and he was intentional. He held them to the mission they had benefitted from and promised to support in

Jerusalem and the rest of the world. This was for the glory of God, the support of the gospel, and the joy of a journey of generosity and giving to others.

Chapter Six

Leading the Team and Yourself

"When it comes at the expense of being respected. According to scientist Cameron Anderson of the Haas School of Business at the University of California, Berkeley, overall happiness in life is related to how much you are respected by those around you. Nevertheless, when we sacrifice what it takes to be respected for the quicker, and often easier, win of feeling liked, we lose out on the benefits that respect yields."[17] – Deborah Grayson Riegel, Leadership Consultant

Whether you have noticed or not, there is leadership depreciation inside of the major fundraising community. Successful leadership skills are important whether you have a small, medium, or large shop. Poor leadership is noticeable everywhere in today's executive culture, but leadership is particularly poor in the Fundraising community, for several reasons.

---

[17] Deborah Grayson Reigel, *Why the Most Successful Leaders Don't Care About Being Liked,* https://www.inc.com/deborah-grayson-riegel/why-most-successful-leaders-dont-care-about-being-liked.html (Inc. Magazine, 2019).

First, many leaders are satisfied with operational teams that are defined as a group of people who are tasked with siloed jobs featuring unilateral decision-making management. In many ways, Fundraising teams are strategically organized like the "spray and pray appeal letter" referenced earlier. "We have a database of 85,000 names so let's write this appeal letter in several different scripts and colors and then send it to our entire list. Send it everywhere and pray a good amount generates from it."

In a previous chapter, I discussed the folly of this strategy because it is fundraising-centric and not donor-centric. The same type of structure has embedded itself in the design of many leadership models and team operations. Sadly, a majority of Fundraising leaders come to the same endgame when hiring, assigning, and leading their team. They hire people, write a job description, assign uncollaborative fundraising goals, and lead a team of siloed associates in hopes that somehow, someway, they will stumble upon collaborative success and meet their subscribed fundraising goals. Intentional organizational leadership does not endorse this format – the leader of such architecture is doomed for failure, as is the mission of the NPO.

Many nonprofits, universities and churches have between three to six people working in their advancement, development, stewardship, or fundraising department. Often, no one is leading, mentoring, or creating a playbook strategy for the department. In the end, poor leadership coincides with poor employee retention, an unintended result of poor leadership.

If you are going to build a relationship with your donors, you can't have a revolving door with your major gift officers. Donors will pick up on the flippant and frenetic organizational structure of your shop or process and lose their passion, or worse yet, their respect for your NPO. I believe poor leadership to be an Achilles heel in fundraising success, especially when you are focused on raising funds for the church. I have discovered that many churches look at fundraising in a similarity to youth ministry. They say, "We have youth so we have to hire a youth pastor and we'll do whatever we can do in youth ministries." The same narrative appears with church boards: "We have tithes and offerings, so we need to hire someone to organize our stewardship and philanthropy for the ministry." They hire an executive pastor with hopes that she, or he, can produce donation growth in the years to come. The executive pastor is then commission with raising their own salary through the parishioners and congregational tithes, offerings, and any additional campaign determined for them. It births another level of high stress turnover within the church's organizational structure. For churches, nonprofits, and universities, the statistics show the average major gift officer lasts about eighteen months. If you probe into the reason for the turnover, fifty percent is because of poor leadership. These MGOs are rarely adequately trained, mentored, or put into a position where they can understand "best practices strategies" and become donor centric. In the previous chapter, I discussed the MGO salary and how you need to pay them in a similar fashion as the private sector. It will take strong leadership to make this needed change in the philanthropic vocation.

I have heard many executives proclaim, "Many of the necessary philosophies of good leadership and team leading can be mentored and developed." I highly disagree with this premise. Instead, leaders need to be identified in respect to their God-given characteristics and skillsets and then you build on those elements. Let me be very clear: Not everyone can be a leader. We need to identify and encourage leadership and take those individuals and develop them as they attend to leading the Fundraising team. If we identify and publicly recognize good leadership, we will be able to retain these leaders within our nonprofits, grow them in their leadership skills and success, and develop a long path of excellence when it comes to successful, organized, donor-centric fundraising.

In Christian universities, presidents usually come from the academic side of higher education. Candidates need to hold at least one PhD, and in many cases, they have earned more than one doctorate. Customarily, a presidential candidate would have first joined the faculty, moved to a dean's position and eventually become a provost before becoming a presidential candidate. In today's higher education culture, this "normal trajectory" into the presidency has radically changed. More and more, future presidents of universities and colleges are coming from the advancement, or fundraising department. It's not only because fundraising and budgeting is a bottom-line revenue, but also because of experienced leadership and the ability to develop relationships with internal colleagues and external constituents. Successful fundraising leaders understand how to organize the team for financial, strategic, and collegial areas of innovative revenue growth and assess human capital margins year after year.

At the time of this writing, Azusa Pacific University (APU) has been without a president for a year and a half due to the unexpected death of long-term President Jon R. Wallace. APU held an official search and determined that Dr. Adam Morris, who has been the vice president of University Advancement at Biola University in La Mirada, California for eighteen years, would serve as its next CEO/President. APU selected a future president who has put together one of the best philanthropy operations in the United States. Adam Morris systematically built Biola's fundraising systems and professional processing leading a fundraising operation with some of the best outcomes in Christ-centered higher education history. This C-suite, professional executive, DNA of a leader is important to the donor, the nonprofit organization, and to future growth. These emerging presidential leaders come from fundraising departments, while many are transitioning into higher education directly from a private sector background and track record.

Weekly I get at least two-to-three phone calls from colleagues at other universities saying: "Eric, I have a situation here with my gift officers…" or "We have a data problem. I've had three guys working data. Should I go back to two?" During these phone calls, I'm also asked organizational questions, emotional intelligence questions, and questions about adjusting and promoting people. The calls and inquiries are a direct result of executive leaders in charge of fundraising teams attempting to understand how to be excellent and professional for the donors, and at the same time, for their staff and for the mission of the nonprofit organization. I appreciate the calls – it's evidence of a passionate leader doing all he or she can to gain skills, strategies, and leadership insights. It is the first step of leadership – a leader's personal sweat equity. Success happens through mature leadership graduating through experiential strategies and processes necessary to build winning leadership skills.

The Beginning of My Leadership Discovery

Ken Hogue, my father, was a blue-collar laborer and tradesman, a stellar sheet metal craftsman, and an eventual (unintentional) business owner. I knew early on that I wasn't going to follow in his footsteps. I have always favored white collar professions that feature employment centered on human capital, organizational development, and projected growth based on investment outcomes. But I learned some valuable leadership characteristics from my father.

First, I believe leadership skills come from God's grace and blessing. I believe leadership is a skill that is given by God to be honed and perfected by the recipient of the gift(s). The second area where you learn how to develop leadership skills is through mentoring. Early in my young life that mentor was my father. In my dad's labor-intensive vocational world, leadership was displayed through his manufactured work. You found it in the finished product, its utilization, and in each client's satisfaction. Dad was a proven and exemplary welder with a self-taught skill of designing custom sheet metal products that companies demanded in mass quantities. His quality in craftsmanship and logistical operational results became his calling card. Every client wanted Ken Hogue to work their metals into perfection.

As my "white collar" professional career began to blossom, I began to comprehend that my father's most desirable colleagues were his arc welder, the metal break, the crimping device, his many clamps, and his God-given ability to design custom blueprints from years of experience in working the metals. He led through a unilateral skillset which produced an expertise that many companies asked for by name. He often said, "Son, when you're welding you must learn to trust the welder's arc to do its job so you can do yours. It's the reason I buy the best welder and I trust it to do the job for me."

Early in my media broadcast career, I was tending to my radio show at WHBC in Canton, Ohio and I received a significant promotion. I was to continue operating my daily radio show, but I was asked to begin to lead a small department and operational component of the station. After the public announcement of my promotion, my dad came to the station and entered the broadcast studio with flowers saying, "Son, I'm really proud of you. When you were younger, I know there was a career choice dissonance between us where, as you know, I wanted you to take over my sheet metal company and you wanted to go into broadcast media. Repeatedly you would tell me, 'Dad, I don't want to be a steel-worker and welder.' I can't lie, it hit my heart pretty hard, as if you were saying you were better than me (my attitude did give this implied message). I want you to know I took what you were saying completely wrong. You are not better than me and I'm not better than you. God has just made us different for different reasons and purposes. In the end, we are both leaders." This is why my father is my favorite communicator, always the "truth-teller" and determined to be a "clear communicator" – even to this day at the age of 82.

Then he continued, "The skillset I have is to lead a construction site, but I lead that team in the vocation and craftsmanship of the job at hand. Now I realize you are gifted to lead teams, people, and something called human capital. You are good at putting people in a job that fits their skills and the projected outcome that needs to be achieved."

At CCU, I have "welders" who are major gift officers. I hire the best and I allow them to do their job under the leadership of our department. My dad would say, "I let the welder do the job, but I make sure I put it to the right angle." There are different types of occupations, but each distinct role within the Fundraising shop requires an acute leadership skill whether it is a planned gift officer working with older donors and their legacy, an annual fund officer working with donors who are just beginning to give to the university, or a major gift officer cultivating a million-dollar gift from a very generous donor. Each of these individuals need to be led, developed, and trained. Each one needs to be comfortable in their job and know what they should be doing and should not be doing. Jim Collins in *Good to Great*, said, "the enemy to being great is settling for just being good."[18] So many times, we accept the current good over the future great. We refuse the hard work, the trusted candor, or the necessary clarity to move from being good to being great – all of this starts and stops with leadership. It takes a commitment to leadership to discover and place your team in the right position. It was Collins

---

[18] Jim Collins, *Good to Great* (New York, NY: HarperCollins, 2001), 1.

who also said, "You must find the right person to be on the right bus in the right seat at the right time for the right job for the right result." In Fundraising, the key is embracing organizational leadership, collegial relationship, and dynamic leadership.

The end does not justify ignoring the obvious. I have had a few encounters where one of my team members, I'll call him David, is in the wrong job because someone put him in the data entry department because they needed a warm body in the data entry post. David is an extrovert and loves to talk with people. There is no one to talk with when you work with data processing systems. The leader needs to notice these "missed positioned roles" and move David into a role that benefits him and the organization. David, ever the socialite, might need to be developed into an event coordinator or an annual fund gift officer where he can meet a large cross-section of donors and represent the NPO's mission to a broad base of new, renewing, and growing donors. To make these critical decisions requires leadership.

I've been in other fundraising shops where somebody comes in and proclaims, "Okay. Our job is to raise eight million dollars. Get out there and do – ask our donors for donations." The team receives no strategic instruction or specialized plan. The bundle of employees embrace the fundraising goal, and they do their best in trying to meet the projection. Eventually, they step on each other as they become frustrated with their inability to achieve any success. Often, this result turns to internal fighting, distracting you (as the leader) and the team with constant emotional waste and conflict resolution. The daily conversation turns from "our wonderful donors" to "our internal personality conflicts and divided atmosphere." This is where the leader needs to understand the necessary leadership applications and instincts needed to bring about calm, clarity, and community, such as external leadership, internal leadership, personal leadership, vertical leadership, and horizontal leadership, which all play into successful fundraising leadership.

Fundraising leadership comes in many fashions, is depicted via various flow charts, and exampled through cutting-edge innovative reforms. But in the end, it is results that are the true test of leadership and the greatest endorsement of a leader. In the vocational, or blue-collar world, leadership is individualized, somewhat siloed in the craftsman's integrity, ethic, and moral authenticity of the project. The tradesmen lead themselves, their projects, bidding, the clients' desired satisfaction, and the overall quality of the designed finished project.

For the executive, leadership is displayed through the results of the team and its processes. To gain these results, the leader uses proven strategies, a focus on results-driven productivity, and most importantly, the sustaining characteristics in you, the leader, as the vision caster.

No matter how you may want to describe non-profit leadership, the ultimate success indicator is found in the various levels of mission-driven results, first for the donor, then your NPO, the fundraising team, and the fundraising leader – in that order of priority. It all comes down to leading teams in successful philanthropic strategies, fundraising perspectives, and strategic leadership.

Warning: Here comes another sports analogy. In many ways, as the director of a Fundraising shop (large or small) you are teaching, mentoring, and coaching your team (players) each day. A successful Fundraising operation details its roster of players, mission-driven philanthropic plays, and designs a clear donor-centric playbook. The coach or leader is constantly putting players in the right position to make the appropriate plays at the appropriate times. As the fiscal year evolves, these players and plays become a strategic playbook of donor-centric systems, processes, and accomplishments.

You must be a logistical leader. In the introduction, I told how my experience as a private sector radio professional prepared me to lead a fundraising team and department at William Jessup University in Rocklin, California. Dr. John Jackson, the president at WJU, knew I had people skills and network connections, and that people knew me and my long tenure as a media persona in Sacramento, CA., but he never considered my 30-plus years of radio logistics would play into a Fundraiser's strategic leadership skillset.

Earlier in this book, I reference the logistical DNA that was forced upon me to be successful in gaining listeners, ratings, retention in listenership, and the ability to be innovative, and to create themes and messaging that brought listeners along in the listening journey. I had to develop a team that performed every day for thousands of listeners. I had to build an audience that produced ratings, active revenue through our sponsors and advertisers, and an allegiance to the station's radio format.

To adapt to thirty years of media changes, I was forced to be innovative and to embrace change whether it was desired change or necessary change. When I started in higher education Fundraising, I did not come from an academic, or university background. Instead, I arrived from the private sector where you had to prove yourself day after day and year after year. My broadcast company focused on performance, with the bottom-line featuring ratings and revenue. To achieve the desired listenership, rating, and client attached revenues to my daily talk show, I created a broadcast structure of proven systems, strategies, and daily logistics to deliver the necessary results for the company.

Organizational leaders are challenged with hiring, developing, and retaining talent while driving business continuity and positioning for future growth and resilience. In a few pages of this book, let me briefly touch upon a small sample of very high-level leadership skillsets necessary for the director, the executive, or the vice president of the NPO's fundraising department and operations.

Playbook Leadership

I've met many philanthropical professionals who are always ready to talk about their leadership theories. If you ask them for specific counsel about how to develop successful leadership, they will give you coded platitudes, coined slogans, and high-level theoretical pontifications.

Here are samples from leading Fundraisers:[19]

- Mr. Thompson thinks leadership is an ability to inspire action for a common cause among diverse groups of people. Inspiring others is the key to success, which she observed during her undergraduate years at the University.

---

[19] Jon Derek Croteau and Zachary A. Smith, *Making the Case for Leadership* (Rowman & Littlefield Publishers, New York, NY, 2012), 84, 85, and 94.

- Mrs. Anderson differentiates leadership from management by describing leadership as more inspirational, or a higher calling to action, and management as the implementation of that call to action.

- Others hold that leadership is very idiosyncratic. There are some very fundamental aspects of it, but most importantly we should try not to make it overly prescriptive. If we do, it might encourage people to look outside of who they really are, rather than within. One joy is working with colleagues who follow their own instinctive paths.

After reading these Fundraising leadership theories, you may feel inspired, but you also ask yourself, "What are the action steps that I need to take to successfully lead my team?" Your question is a good one because inspirational leadership is great for emotional collegiality, but it contributes nothing to actual achievement and measurable fundraising success.

Fundraising leadership needs a long-term commitment to sound logistics or a leadership style that determines and employs the necessary "blocking and tackling" of the job, donor-centric strategies, and the hard work of a strategizing leader for the Fundraising department. The Bible tells us that people without a vision will perish. In a similar manner, the Fundraiser without a clear strategy will languish.

Jerry A. May is one of my "go to" Advancement professionals. I'll admit to a love-hate relationship with Jerry's career. Jerry has served as vice president of development at the University of Michigan and THE Ohio State University. As an expatriate of the great state of Ohio and a lifelong Buckeye fan, I believe Jerry's tenure in Ann Arbor is best described as an apprenticeship and his tenure in Columbus, Ohio as the crown jewel of his professional achievement. Jerry May has been an iconic philanthropic figure for both institutions and a frequent Advancement strategic leader for public and private higher education.

May states, "I think that leadership is not only about taking responsibility, but it is taking an organization, team, or program to a new level of performance."[20] For May, leadership moves an organization beyond just the people and their talents toward larger goals and objectives.

May believes leadership has three types:[21]

1. **Leading by position** – where you help others maximize their capabilities.

2. **Leading by facilitating** – the delegation of upward movement and bandwidth.

3. **Leading by stimulating leadership** – the leader has no immediate control or leverage. May calls on benchmarking data, outside consultants, special ideation strategy sessions, and outside volunteers to get involved and stimulate a direction or a change.

May describes his three general leadership areas saying, "It takes hard work. It's about building meaningful relationships, but it's also about developing a strategic plan and holding yourself and your team accountable."[22]

---

[20] Croteau and Smith, Making the Case for Leadership, 115.
[21] Ibid, 121-122.
[22] Ibid, 125.

While I agree with May's niche segmented effort, I also believe there is an additional step, one that is more granular, more elementary in detail, one that describes the distinct blocking and tackling of Fundraising leadership. I like black and white, microscopic clarity that details the necessary plays needed for the whole of the Fundraiser's playbook success. Don't give me theories, pontifications, or mystic platitudes. Instead, create, design, and describe an actual instructional manual.

A Few Tangible Fundamentals

Practical leadership involves the necessity for implementation. You can talk about it forever with few results, but implementation of these fundamentals is key. Here are several areas of implementation and leadership:

1. **Design Meeting Agendas for Results and Decisions.** When I run and facilitate a meeting, the day before the meeting, I provide the agenda which is written, emailed, and features topic assignments. As the lead facilitator of the agenda during the meeting, I control topics, the timing to prevent chasing squirrels (or rabbit trails), and any corporate red herring discussions. As a vice president, I'm not removed from my team during the meeting but collegial in leading my team through the agenda. With a granular meeting agenda with substance which addresses problems, I drive each agenda item to a decision. If it is impossible to reach a decision, I assign the necessary next step ideation or group implementation and ask for a "report back" on the next meeting's agenda. As the leader, you are the quarterback,

you are calling the plays and signaling any actions needed for the tasks determined to be necessary and ready for implementation. The agenda is not a template, but rather a living and breathing document that must measure progress, welcome innovation(s), and attend to problem solving items as needed. I set ninety-minute meetings with five to eight agenda items. The number of agenda items depends on who is attending. As you know your team, you will know which person is a talker and who is not. Also, you'll know which agenda items need more time and then you can narrow it to three items. For example, on a Monday I create the agenda for a Tuesday meeting with my major gift officers. I know if the agenda moves quickly, then we can have eight items but if not completed, then those items will be first and second, the next time we get together. During the meeting, we talk about the last agenda and determine if we are implementing or need to do additional discussion. As the lead facilitator you have to make these types of decisions and you can't let the meeting determine your pace or outcome.

2. **Lead by Example**. When it comes to assigning the necessary team tasks, policy, or determining processes, as the leader, I try to get my contact reports in first. I schedule donor visits and other communications as fast as I can. In different ways, I show my team what I'm doing. Even as a university vice president, I'm doing the day-to-day or week-to-week tasks that I am expecting of them. My projections and my gift-pledge proposals are public. I'm using every donor-centric technique that I know as an

example and expect my team to do the same work. When you lead through your personal example, there is a lot of comfort in these actions. The Apostle Paul told us, "Do as I do" when he was talking about the commitment to faith and righteousness. Just as Paul challenged himself in leading the church, I commit myself to the same path in leading my team. It's inappropriate for me to come into a team portfolio meeting and say, "I want you to do contact reports but I'm not going to do them." I've found that my sweat equity creates a collegial team that is focused and celebratory when they accomplish their goals and projections. The phrase "lead by example" is a flippant phrase, but you must do it – every single day!

As you know from a previous chapter, one my favorite leadership phrases to defeat a temptation to micromanage is to constantly repeat the phrase I need to "inspect what I expect." In the fashion, as the leader, you must commit yourself to being the example of what is prescribed, requested, and instructed from your leadership. At the same time, you need to have a welcoming candor to hear the same phrase asked of you from time-to-time. You must have respect for those around you, and valuing others enough to give them honest feedback when they ask about desired outcomes that originate from your desk.

High-performing chief advancement officers and executive directors understand the notion that success happens when preparation and opportunity are in alignment. They take responsibility for the success of their organization and expect the same of their team, staff, or subordinates. They understand they have a responsibility to project leadership by the nature of their position, but they also know when they must lead behind the scenes by facilitating the work of others. They are not afraid to get their hands dirty, and they seek to establish credibility by being engaged, available, and actively involved (inspect what you expect) in the day-to-day work of the organization.

3. **Prescribe "Inverted 1x1 Meetings."** In addition to these team meetings, I schedule bi-monthly individual meetings. This is nothing new; most leaders will have one-on-one meetings with their staff either on a weekly or bi-weekly basis. These meetings are an opportunity to meet with your director of data donor services, director of strategic philanthropy, senior director of major gifts or director of planned giving. During this meeting, you check in, give them a chance to clear the air and get some updates. Where my meetings feature a different focus is by inverting the whole process. For my 1x1s I ask my direct reports to schedule a 30-minute meeting with me every other week. The director brings their agenda to me, determining what they believe I need to know about their projects, successes, and roadblocks. It's inverted because I don't determine or create the agenda; my direct reports do. The directors know they have my attention and my ear for thirty undistracted minutes to talk about problems or successes or whatever they want. Usually, they have three or four items on their agenda. As the leader, you listen, question, and

take copious notes. These inverted one-on-one meetings allow you, as the department leader, to know how your staff is prioritizing their day-to-day activities, learn of their dilemmas, and how they think, and create intradepartmental remedies as well as logistically strategize solutions. With these meetings, I have one caveat where the meeting may go forty-five minutes – if I have something immediate to ask of them. It is rare. If I do schedule a one-on-one meeting with them, then they know there is a problem and a one topic issue that will be discussed in-depth, and they are not ambushed.

4. **Learn to be an Emotional Intelligence (EI) Leader.** In today's world where Human Resources (HR) is involved in everything you do as a manager or an executive in a large company organization, you must have emotional intelligence. You must be able to read a room. You will learn the skilled EI characteristics that you have or must develop to make precise decisions. Most leaders hate this part of the job as it includes conflict resolution or reprimanding behavior with corrective instruction. EI involves communicating what you expect and then being clear about the adjustments you want if the activity does not reach the standard that the team needs. This is where experience is vital. As the leader you must grow in professionalism, personal maturity, clarity, authenticity, conflict resolution, and personal morality or character. I believe EI to be an obtained skillset. You can teach yourself to trust your EI senses, discernment, and conclusions.

The majority of this area involves egos being stepped on. For employees who have a certain perception of themselves or when they hear direct candor in a meeting, they may take it personally. When this happens, it can become a bit dicey within the team.

We are in a staff meeting and Patti says, "I'm tired of doing the dishes in the kitchen." On the other side of the table, Bill says, "We've been traveling and meeting with donors and it's tough for us to get to these housekeeping tasks. We will do our best."

Later, Patti put up a sign in the kitchen, "Your mother doesn't work here." She is a little more perturbed and has an office sedimentary job and believes cleaning the kitchen has fallen on her because she doesn't travel and takes offense telling me, "I'm not cleaning up the kitchen again." Then she offers, "I see a bit of sexism here because you boys don't clean up after yourselves and you think we women should do it."

As a leader, whether you like it or not, you have an immediate issue which must be handled. You need the emotional intelligence to understand both perspectives of the issue. To you, it may seem like a remedial issue, but if you don't step in and handle it, it will grow worse rapidly. As a leader you must address the episode right away and handle it correctly. Because of the "human condition" the event or issue(s) will go beyond your team and eventually reach the donors. As a regrettable example, some MGO is going to lunch with a donor, and they talk about the university, the fundraising department, and their professional colleagues and something very human is going to be uttered, "Our team is good except for the guys who think the women have to do all the work at the office." It's offered flippantly – even humorously – no matter, it has now reached the donors and the external community. You don't want these types of conversations to go beyond your team, into your donor relations, and being to impact your leadership. You must address it quickly, collegially, and with great candor and transparency. The directive from your desk is to discuss it fully, honestly, and clearly, and to arrive at a clearing conversation and declare the issue resolved "as of today," and you move on – lead forward.

To handle these situations, the leader has to skillfully use emotional intelligence and be willing to make very clear decisions and proclamations.

You will need to grow this leadership muscle. The human condition is a trusted default position in evaluating team members. Human ego is real and dependable. Human territorial fears are woven into the performing workplace and can become phycological realities for mid-level directors and their groups. The broken reality of human personal lives will enter the workplace and impact group dynamics so you should plan for it. Character flaws such as jealousy, half-truths, arrogance, braggadocio, and weak temperance will become common opponents to your team's success and collegial meter.

Nobody says, "I love conflict." The truth is everyone hates it and dislikes dealing with it. But it is a real human condition that repeatedly surfaces in your team. Your EI skillset will give you leading indicators that preclude the public arrival of conflict. These types of challenges will never be deterred until through your leadership, it is lanced, the festering is forced to the surface, and then each item of irritation is addressed, defined, and remedied.

5. **Be a Skillful Self-effacing Leader.** Boulder, Colorado resident Jim Collins' famous book *Good to Great* is still, in my opinion, one of the best leadership books on the market. Collins' book balances between theory and actionable which is something most leadership books do not achieve.

   I distinctly remember Collins book's 2001 debut. At that time, I was working as a local and regional talk radio host for Salem Radio Network (SRN, now Salem Media). My direct SRN executive leadership featured two senior vice presidents, Joe Davis and Ken Gaines. During my frequent meetings with both of these C-Suite leaders, they expressed their constant admiration for Collins' work in *Good to Great*. Eventually, Collins' book became a company-wide mandatory read for each Salem executive and market cluster general manager.

The opening sentence of Collins' book says, "Good is the enemy of great. And that is one of the key reasons why we have so little that becomes great."[23] He immediately talks about breakthrough growth and organizational success as he addresses the leader's weaknesses, skillsets, and desired personal growth.

To begin Chapter Two, Collins' offers a Harry S. Truman quote, "You can accomplish anything in life, provided that you do not mind who gets the credit."[24] This quote leads the reader into Collins' contract of the *Level 5 Manager*. Notice how Collins states the obvious: If you want to move your team from good to great, it begins with you, the leader. It begins with your preparation, your attitude, and your ego. Collins states, "Level 5 leaders channel their ego needs away from themselves and into the larger goal of building a great company. It's not that Level 5 leaders have no ego or self-interest. Indeed, they are incredibly ambitious, but their ambition is first and foremost for the institution, not themselves."[25] He then takes after (1) the executive, (2) the leader, (3)the manager, (4) team member, and (5) the capable individual.

As a leader you don't care who gets the credit because as the leader you want the department to get the credit. My second year at Colorado Christian University was the first time we raised eight million dollars comprehensively within one fiscal year. We hired a lot

[23] Jim Collins, Good to Great
[24] Ibid,
[25] Jim Collins, Good to Great, 21

of people who made a lot of changes, which is the playbook. Some of the gift officers came in and they had great success with donors giving large gifts. Two other gift officers had a good year but just not this level of success. During this time there was constant praise tossed to Bob and Katy. The other two gift officers, Sally and Michael, sat back and they would chime in but after a while this situation became a bit of an irritant for them. They felt bad like they didn't do their job. I sensed the room.

Later I brought Michael and Sally into the office and asked, "Is there a problem?"

"Yes, I wish we could have done better," Michael began.

Sally nodded her head and said, "Bob has a nice portfolio and mine is still being cultivated."

I reassured them that is not the case, and no one is thinking that way. "Also, this is just one fiscal year." From that meeting, I changed the university advancement team nickname to the "A Team" like the old TV show. Now for every success, we thank God for his provision and success for the A team, *and then* we'll talk about individual people who had a hand in it. I rebranded our internal language to talk about our team, not as a group of individuals, but as the A team. Because when Bob brings in a gift, Matthew does the processing of the check and the data and prepares the thank you card with the receipt. It is the A Team which was successful.

A self-effacing leader puts himself or herself in the mix. I never come in and say I just went out to lunch and a four-million-dollar gift came in. Instead, I say, "Hey A Team, I had a donor generously fulfill a $4 million pledge. Way to go." When we celebrate monthly blessings or successes, we do it as a team. If your birthday is in a quarter, as a team we go to lunch and celebrate. I stopped the individualistic evaluations within the team and made it collegial and wholistic including for myself. Collins talks about level five leaders: the executive, the leader, the manager, the team member, and the capable individual. All of those areas have to be in me, so it is replicated in the team.

I've walked into some university shops where on a whiteboard in the kitchen, they have what everyone has raised beside their projection. That doesn't happen with my team. I hand out one comprehensive report with the fundraising dollars that have come from our generous donors through the A Team for the mission at Colorado Christian University. No one's name is on that report. I know who may or may not be hitting their projected goals, but I do not mention it publicly. The goal is to get your colleagues to think "donor, team, NPO, mission, and success" before self.

Evaluate Your Performance. Every year I create 20 to 25 questions about my leadership. I have my executive assistant, Jill, email them to my team who fills them out and return them. I don't see them, but Jill offers me the aggregate return of the survey. The questions are about how I lead, how I manage, my integrity, my character, clarity, and trustworthiness. They evaluate via five different ranges like "never, sometimes, always," etc. My colleagues fill out the survey and have the ability to make open comments. All of the data comes back to me through Jill and is kept confidential. I use this information to evaluate myself. At times, I've laid some of the information in front of my university president or the director of human resources. I want them to look at it with me so I'm not just leading the team and evaluating their leadership. I'm also evaluating my leadership.

Here are a few of the survey questions I offer myself to each year:

- ➢ How satisfied are you with the management style of your direct manage (VP)?
- ➢ Do you believe your direct manager has the expertise and competence to help you and your team succeed?
- ➢ On a scale from 1 to 5, how confident are you in the overall effectiveness of your direct manager?
- ➢ I feel comfortable voicing concerns toward my direct manager.
- ➢ My direct manager is approachable.
- ➢ How responsive is your direct manager to ideas, requests, and suggestions?
- ➢ How professionally does your direct manager handle disagreements?
- ➢ My direct manager recognizes the importance of my personal and family life.
- ➢ I feel that my manager has an interest in my professional development.
- ➢ How clearly does your manager explain tasks to you?
- ➢ How well does your direct manager communicate expectations?
- ➢ My direct manager motivates me to do my best work.
- ➢ I regularly receive meaningful feedback on my work from my direct manager.

➢ The deadlines set by my direct manager are real.

➢ My direct manager always explains the reasons behind the decisions made within the organization.

➢ How aligned are your direct manager's priorities with your organization's goals?

➢ My direct manager has the organization's best interest in mind.

➢ My manager takes responsibility for his/her actions.

➢ My direct manager reinforces strengths instead of weakness.

➢ My direct manager treats everyone in the office equally.

➢ My direct manager does not display favoritism.

➢ What could your direct manager do to improve?

I cannot express how valuable it is for my team members to receive a personal review rubric from me, about me, and my leadership characteristic. Not only does it help me to make immediate adjustments, but it will help me lead intermittently through the year. In my leadership I love direct candor versus dancing around issues. When I have to adjust, correct, or mentor a team member, and I bring them into my office for the encounter, they always reference my annual self-review and thank me for my candor, the clarity, and the clear directive(s).

Grow your Competency. It's been said "readers are leaders". My usual reading features leadership, philanthropy, Scripture, and my fun places where I read biographies of sports, political and historical legends, and heroes. My reading on leadership is not so much as what

I need to do for my team, as what I need to do for myself. As a leader, when you work to develop yourself, you will eventually turn this effort into one that includes your team and colleagues.

The Fundraising leader position is not for everyone, and no one, at the outset of accepting the leader's post, is completely ready for the job. You must understand that your leadership post is a work in progress and your competency as a leader must be developed.

Competency simply means to do something successfully or efficiently. In this position there is a duality of competency. Every leader must perform with competency and lead with competency. What follows are a number of areas where the fundraising leader needs to achieve competency.[26]

Intellectual Curiosity: I'm curious about everything. Recently I received an email from William Jessup University on their "Give 24" campaign. I went to their giving site, then to the bottom of their giving page to see who built it for them. Then I researched the company to see which other universities were using this platform. Next, I grabbed an aggregate of those various universities and did a comparison between small, medium, and large and I noticed how they were doing with their online giving days. I made this effort out of my own curiosity. I want to know who is doing what and how they are doing it, and then compare it to our efforts and see if we can improve our results.

Lifelong learning is vital for any leader. I have more books on my shelf to be read than I have actually read. And I have even more book futures loaded into my Amazon wish list bucket. My wife believes I

---

[26] Croteau and Smith, Making the Case for Leadership, 191-200.

have a *book hoarding* problem. Effective leaders in philanthropy focus on staying current with the profession, the cultural demographics of donors, and their nonprofit organization. I believe self-improvement starts with observing others success, emulating leadership qualities you desire to build, and paying attention to poor leadership so you can make every attempt to remove the negative qualities from your leadership playbook.

I always question everything. For example, in the area of appeal letters, in 2022, I wondered: "Should we be sending snail mail to 30-year-olds? Is it vital and successful? Do millennials or even GenZ want physical mail, and do they even go to their mailbox? I know they open emails." The process comes from my curiosity.

Professional Communicator: Earlier in this book I stated that every major gift officer hired needed to be a good written communicator. The leader needs to be an excellent communicator, writer, and speaker. As a leader, I regularly speak at Kiwanis, Rotary, and chamber of commerce meetings so I can practice my speaking. I put myself in different arenas so my speaking stays sharp. You need to listen well, and communicate in clear, concise, and appropriate ways. You need to understand your audience: to whom you are communicating such as to an individual, group, or a crowd and employ the right decorum needed for that room's audience. You need to articulate the NPO's mission and vision better than anyone else on your team because you are the leader. You need to promote equality, transparency, authenticity, and external professionalism in every mode of communication.

Self-awareness: You need to be an expert of *you*. The best leaders are those who are keenly aware of their strengths and weaknesses. This affords you the confidence to hire team members who compliment your professional areas of weakness. Leaders must be confident in their own skin, but aggressive slayers of the ego. Our egos are alive, and they are good – within a certain arena. But you need to be honest with yourself about how controlling your ego is on your leadership passion(s), decisions, and your holistic ambitions and personal achievements. A mature leader looks out the window and not into a mirror. You look out the window for direction and strategy, as well as to give appropriate credit for the success of the organization to your team members and the successful work they are accomplishing. You look in the mirror to evaluate critique.

As of this writing, Tammy and I have been married for 34 years. Early in our marriage I was not very self-aware, but I continue to grow in this area as a leader (and as a husband). I had been on my own since I was 18 and knew how to make decisions for myself -- but not always for my marriage and family. I had blind spots and needed to be more self-aware to adjust. In fact, everything I've highlighted in this book as action steps came because I worked through a blind spot and adjusted.

Critical Thinker: Exercise these three traits: personal leadership reflection, honest critical analysis, and scheduling calendar time to think and ideate toward innovation and implementation.

You must protect your time to think!

Regardless of your business, you must manage yourself first. Set aside time to think, ideate, reflect upon past decisions, evaluate outcomes, and consider adjustments and new concepts. Refuse the temptation to be drawn into the "daily crises" and manage them according to their actual priorities. Word of encouragement: sometimes a staff fire, or a fire drill, is meant to burn for a while. Don't feel compelled to run to the fires and soak them with water to douse emotions. Let them burn off the chaff so you can get to the core issue(s). Pay attention to what is vital to the organization and the success of your team's purpose. Finally, you need to work at your negotiation skills, improve them, and be "savvy" in practical knowledge and your ability to make good judgments. You need to gain common sense in your decision making. If you are a successful leader your decision-making process, time, and weight (not always volume) will never relent. Be prepared for this reality!

Organizational Guru: When I came to Colorado Christian University, my office had only a small 3' x 4' whiteboard. I called facilities and said, "I need large whiteboards on both these walls."

The campus facilities director said, "Mr. Hogue, you want both of these walls to be a whiteboard from ceiling to floor?" I nodded my yes. "You want it painted with that whiteboard paint." Again, I nodded yes.

"One more thing," I said, "Please paint it so it can have a magnet behind it."

"What is that for?" he asked.

"I like to stick things on the whiteboard when I write on it."

He laughed and said, "We've never had anyone ask for this. Bookcases? Sure. Curtains? Yes. Nice conference table? No problem.

But a floor to ceiling whiteboard across from the windows so the light will shine on it? That is a unique request."

I am a visual learner, thinker, and innovator – I need to see it when I think it. I will spend time in my office looking at our organizational chart and job descriptions of our employees. I will innovate and create and then read books on organizational structure. I read books on shipping companies like Roadway because these companies have to travel out, meet a client, then either make a pickup or a delivery. I compare that to my work as a gift officer working with my donors. On my current whiteboard wall I have our current organizational chart featuring twelve people, a five-year chart with twenty-eight people and a ten-year chart with fifty-two people. They are on a whiteboard so I can easily erase and change them.

Your organization represents living breathing humans who are successful, donor-centric, mission-centric, and focused on raising money so the university or nonprofit grows. Nothing is static. I'm growing as a leader. Our organization is growing in people, enrollment is growing, and our cabinet is growing. If you think you can have an organizational chart on a piece of paper which has been there five years, you are not growing nor planning to grow.

I work for a higher education organization. We offer programs for students wanting to earn an undergraduate and/or graduate degree in organizational management. I am often amazed at how inept colleges and universities can be in designing organizational success for themselves. At times, it embarrasses me. We have lead faculty members who are teaching these constructs to students and we, the teaching expert(s), cannot follow the best practices, appropriate structure, or the niche instructions we are offering to our customers. Let me be clear: If you are a C-Suite executive leader, you MUST become an organizational guru! You must focus on building a positive and productive organizational structure and culture. You must continually assess and evaluate your organizational structure in order to make changes, adjustments, and additions where and when necessary.

I am a super fan of the distributed leadership model within my department. As fast as you can, create a hierarchy of leadership within your department (small or large) and begin to mentor leadership within your team as you pass off responsibilities. In a future book I hope to detail my idea of distributed leadership organizational models for philanthropic success. Briefly, you need to locate team members who are able, asking, and desiring to become a leader within your organizational chart. Give them a seat at the "Leadership Team" table and announce their placement before the whole team. Assign areas of leadership, invite them into problem solving, strategies, discussions of department policies, and ideation sessions for increased success and future opportunities. You must constantly build your organizational flow chart, always thinking of ways to develop leaders, improve leadership, enhance organizational culture, and the operating environment of your department and team members.

Focused on Professionalism and Excellence

These are my two favorite words. If you pull Matthew, my director of data, aside and ask, "What are Eric's favorite words?"

He would say, "Professionalism and excellence."

If you pull Nancy aside, our director of strategic philanthropy, and asked, "What does Eric expect?"

"He wants excellence and professionalism."

If you pulled Derek aside, our annual fund officer, and asked, "What does Eric expect?"

"Excellence and professionalism."

These two words of excellence and professionalism are in our meeting rooms, our agendas. And when we make decisions, they are our filters. We are called to excellence and professionalism. God called us a peculiar people because we care about excellence and professionalism as these qualities speak to the other person and not just me. It's a matter of living our lives inside out so we are excellent for the donors and the mission, and then professional about how we handle the job at Colorado Christian University.

Why Leadership Is Important

This topic is critical for today's culture. Every week we are hearing stories about Christian leaders who stumble in their leadership with a moral failure. When I hear of these tragedies, I wonder, *where is the leadership?*

We have all seen examples of leadership which are myopic, self-centered, and self-aggrandizing. These traits don't contribute to the good of the mission or glory of God or the betterment of mankind. Our unseen enemy -- and our human condition -- will constantly tell us to think of ourselves as a god of our own. The first temptation came from a tree of the knowledge of good and evil. That's why excellent and professional leadership is so important for the church, nonprofit ministries, and Christian universities.

Chapter Seven

Underestimating Women Philanthropists

"To build relationships on behalf of your cause, do a lot of listening. You will grow as a person, but you will also learn what giver cares about deeply." – Dr. Mark Dillon, *Giving & Getting in the Kingdom*[27]

Women and Philanthropy

In recent American history over the last thirty to forty years, women are making more of the decisions about philanthropy. During, the last two years at CCU, women's representation in the university's major donor base has grown 35%. Some of the variables accounting for this change are cultural acceptance, duality with household incomes, equality in pay, and the glass ceilings being shattered. As more women become CEOs and increase their wealth, they are more willing to be engaged in philanthropy and a leading role in donor demographics.

---

[27] Mark Dillon, *Giving & Getting in the Kingdom* (Moody Press, Chicago 2012), 63.

Men and women handle money in different ways. Some of the well-known iconic investors are men named Merrill Lynch, Goldman, Sachs, and Schwab. Until recently, the same pattern has held true for philanthropy. If you research the list of philanthropists who have signed *The Giving Pledge*, sprinkled among the men (and couples) mentioned are a population of individual women philanthropists -- names such as Sue Ann Arnall, Sara Blakely, Judy Faulkner, Melinda Gates, and Lyda Hill.

Researchers have discovered women are better investors than men. Fidelity analysis covered 5.2 million customers accounts from 2011 to 2020. Their research covered individual retirement accounts, 529 plans, and basic brokerage accounts. A fact never reported or understood is women outperformed men in every category. The source of women's superior returns is the way they trade or better stated, it's the way they don't trade. Women Fidelity traders bought and sold half as much as men. In a classic paper that appeared in the *Journal of Finance* in 2000, titled "Trading is Hazardous to your Wealth," the research proved that investors who traded the most earned an annual return that was 6.5 percentage points worse than the overall performance of the stock market.

Men love to buy and trade frenetically, and women do not. There are a number of assumed "cultural and social predictors." I want to highlight what I believe to be the real reasons behind the comparative success women have over men with investing and demonstrate that same logic and skillset through women and philanthropy.

In a predominantly man's world which is changing, Manisha Thakor, a financial planner and founder of MoneyZen in Portland,

Oregon, stated, "Women are socialized to be perfect, to know everything before we take a step." Thakor followed up during a TED Talk, "Men are more comfortable making decisions without knowing everything." I find Thakor's opinion very interesting. She is making a direct comparison to male donors who give without a greater necessity to hear back of the impact or outcome of their giving. On the other hand, women are slower to give, but when they do make a philanthropic gift (or commitment) they expect a timely report on the impact and outcomes expected and expressed at the time of the gift.

For whatever reason, historically, men have been dominant in finances. I will chalk this up to experience and confidence. But things are changing, which means women involved in philanthropy are changing Fundraising practices. If we believe the evidence, that women prove to be better investors than men, then we best believe they will be better (or different) philanthropists too. I have embraced this cultural trend as a reality and because I have helped a number of leading ladies deliver their philanthropy to and through higher education, here are a few of my characteristic observations:

1. Women research more than men when making major donations.
2. Women are NOT risk takers with their philanthropy.
3. Women demand more from the NPO recipient in proven outcomes.
4. Women want to know, with detail, the impact that their gifts will accomplish.

5. Women are more niche; they desire a distinct conduit of giving.

6. Women are more individually sustainable. And when they commit to a large gift, they remain committed to the NPO and the outcomes – and they will be vocal about any/all shortcomings.

Within the general fundraising community, I've observed this significant shift and growing trend and I believe it merits a focused chapter to highlight perspectives, practices, and processes that Fundraisers will need to make for philanthropic success in the years ahead.

I have heard of stories where major gift officers have underestimated, patronized or worse yet they have "gaslighted" their philanthropic encounters with lead philanthropic women in their portfolios. Professional colleagues have told me about male MGOs who make the grave mistake of approaching female philanthropists with a "chauvinistic jaundice," which is nothing more than a predetermined stereotype that "these rich women need my help with their philanthropic decision making because they did not personally earn their wealth, or it was inherited, and they have no idea how to determine their philanthropic passions and strategies."

Let me be clear – this is a huge mistake!

At a recent Fundraising conference, I overheard a major gift officer say to a table full of national male fundraising professionals, "Cultivating women is an opportunity, as an experienced major gift officer you can easily manipulate recent widows into making large gifts by focusing on their husband's passing, legacy, and utilizing emotional ploys." I reacted with amazement and shock – no one pushed back or challenged the comment or its implied premise: "Play upon the emotions of the woman. Remind her of her husband's wealth and his desires on how to utilize 'his philanthropic wishes from the grave.' "

When I heard this comment and the ensuing dialogue, it sounded, to me at least, like mind-games tactics of Jack Manningham who was the main character, in the 1938 play *Gaslight* by Patrick Hamilton. The movie offers a twisted husband, Jack, who treats his wife, Bella, as a lesser light, reinforcing stereotypes of secondary intelligence. Throughout the play, Jack's temper fluctuates constantly then he dismisses and belittles Bella through a constant argument of what is and is not reality in Bella's head as he turned lights on and off trying to convince her that she was going mad. The classic movie is acute in its portrayal of psychological domestic abuse and toxic masculinity.

The concept of *gaslighting* is a colloquialism described as a means of making someone question their own reality, ability, or identity. In a few ways, I've seen major gift officers who employ this technique, usually unintentionally.

As a tenured husband of thirty-four years and a father of two strong-willed daughters, I have heard these subjective narratives in numerous cultural settings. Within Fundraising, the benchmark ideology is that the male, the traditional breadwinner, is always the lead when it comes to making philanthropic decisions. Afterall, he earned it, and it is his to decided. Included in these false assumptions related to finances is that men know better, they aren't emotional about money and are in a better state of mind to handle the brash, black and white decisions involving money management. I am not saying that MGOs intentionally operate in a way to cause harm to women philanthropists, but many MGOs consider women as inexperienced, non-bread winners, unfamiliar with how to make major donations and major monetary decisions.

One episode of this reality features a very experienced and tenured MGO in my former office. He had a significant portfolio that featured many older couples who had supported the university for a number of years, some of them for decades. The Pattersons were very active, older aged, donors in his portfolio. On a summer afternoon, Neal received a phone call and was informed about David Patterson's passing. This news of an unexpected death made a significant impact on Neal.

Neal visited me in my office to share the news and proceeded to share his concerns about the Pattersons moving forward in further support of the university. I could see the concern on Neal's face and hear it in his voice, so I asked him why he was so concerned.

Neal said, "Eric, David was the patriarch of that family. He made all of the philanthropic decisions. He knew finance and was a successful market investor right up until he passed last week."

I asked Neal, "What concerns you so much?"

Neal responded with great certainty, "Maggie is not going to be able to discuss future donations and the completion of their five-year capital campaign pledge. I don't think it is in her wheelhouse. In time I will need to build a connection with their older son, David Jr., to discuss the Pattersons' passions, intents, and planned gifts."

I pressed him, "What makes you believe Maggie cannot have these conversations with you, of course, in time? She may surprise you."

While somewhat reluctant, Neal decided to schedule an initial meeting with Maggie, and he made the meeting three months after David's passing, the funeral, and family memorial services. When Neal and Maggie finally met, he was caught off-guard with her preparations, knowledge of their philanthropic pledge and planned gifts. During their meeting, Maggie asked to adjust a few things with their pledge so David's passions could be accomplished sooner via his life insurance policy.

Neal was amazed. I was pleased that he gave Maggie the time to prove herself in the initial meeting. Neal eventually respected her enough to see her as an equal partner of David's. His ability to move from assumption, stereotype, and an attitude of patronizing Maggie taught him a personal lesson and saved a key donor for the university. Can you imagine if Neal had acted on his initial perception and assumptions?

Where do these misconceptions about women occur in everyday life? The best example I can offer is from experience. My wife and our daughters have all been interrupted by car problems. I am not a car mechanic. I try, but it's not in my skillset (remember my father's white versus blue collar reality). In a relatable marketplace comparison, a good analogy is my recollection of my wife and daughters interacting with auto mechanics at a garage or a salesman at a car dealership. It's easy to get to the immediate stereotypes, when a woman talks about an automobile, a man quickly assumes she does not know what she is talking about, asking for, or paying for. I have heard this from my wife in reference to her car needing repairs or attention from a mechanics garage:

- You call, they will respond to a male voice versus a female voice.

- It's a mechanics garage, they will play me for the fool and confuse me.

- I want to decide my choice of new car, but I need you to go because I don't want to be played.

As this relates to fundraising and philanthropy, the culture is gradually adjusting for women in the corporate world, pay equality, and particularly in philanthropic circles. The culture is also embracing more and more women as philanthropic leaders, strategists, and inspectors of sound outcomes and impacts.

In many ways, it is women who are the future's leading wealth engineers of philanthropy. I reference major donor Lisa Greer once again, "The 'ladies who lunch' have been around forever. But consider this: the report *'Women and Million Dollar Giving: Current Landscape and Trends to Watch'* found that in high-net-worth households, 84% of women are the primary decision-maker or joint decision-maker regarding investments. Women were also identified in the report as being twice as likely to view charitable giving as the most satisfying aspect of wealth, and also more likely to value their wealth as a way to create positive change[28]."

The media has been telling us about the "Great American Wealth Transfer" coming in the near future. It is estimated that this historic

---

[28] Lisa Greer, Philanthropy Revolution, 88.

wealth transfer will feature a total of $68 trillion from one generation to the next in the coming years. I am here to inform you that this wealth transfer is already underway!

This wealth will be transferred to heirs, charities, and taxes. The Center on Wealth and Philanthropy at Boston College (2014), estimates that from 2007 to 2061 close to $27 trillion will be bequest to charities, $53 trillion to heirs, and $8 trillion to taxes.

During a recent seminar CCU and the Denver Seminary hosted with the National Christian Foundation (NCF), Jeanne McMains, the senior vice president for NCF's Northwest Seattle Office, proclaimed that this historic wealth transfer is going to witness women growing in a dominant philanthropic influence, and particularly women who are millennials.

It's estimated that women will inherit 70% of the great wealth transfer. In essence, women will be responsible for two-thirds of the nation's wealth by 2030.

Seventy-five percent of households feature women managing the income and budget. The transfer will feature two-thirds, or close to 70% of women managing the inheritance come 2030 and beyond.

Philanthropy is philanthropy; it is the fuel to produce your desired outcomes, impacts, and personal passion(s). Planned gifts represent future fuel to produce legacy outcomes, family inheritance passions, and long-term guidelines. There is nothing male or female about philanthropy. The past several years have proven that there is one philanthropy and women are poised to play a very significant – if not lead role – in all areas of philanthropic futures.

Here are a few realities for women and philanthropy:

1.　Women are executives and/or C-suite leaders in corporate America.

2.　Women handle the household's budget, investments, and financial planning.

3.　Women inherited family wealth through equity in sibling bequests (it used to be, a majority – if not all – of parental legacy inheritance was left for the boy/men, of the family).

4.　The more philanthropy is operated like a growth managed organization or investment, the more women will be attracted to its philanthropic outcomes and missional impact(s) versus strict altruism.

5.　Women are attracted to the "cultural remedies" that guide niche (leading) missions of NPOs, versus the year-over-year operational growth and P&L spread sheets of public companies and shareholder investing.

6.　More women than men increase their annual giving the following year if the NPO's mission remedy is being addressed and producing a desirable outcome(s).

7.　Women seek in-depth learning of their choice NPO and its remedy mission, so they fully engage with the NPO that fits their giving goals.

8.　Women trust faster and deeper (once trust is established), as they desire the community of an NPO's donor base. Giving circles are broadened as they invite other women to join them and participate.

The Women's Philanthropy Institute (WPI) was interested in exploring the high number of women who participate in crowdfunding.[29] The initial research discovered that women are drawn to both collective giving and non-traditional forms of philanthropy. In a 2021 report entitled *Gender and Crowdfunding*, one of the seven key findings surrounding the motivation for women and crowdfunding philanthropy was that women believe a gift will make a difference or to remedy issues close to them and their lives.[30]

When it comes to the stock market, overconfidence is bad, and women are less likely to fall victim to it. *Denver Post* writer Ron Lieber states in a January 2022 column *(New York Times, Spending Well, Denver Post Sunday Insert, January 2022, p.38W)*, "Researchers have found women to be the better investors." Lieber's researched report reveals that it is not how women invest, it is how they don't. Female Fidelity investors bought and sold half as much as their male counterparts. He also states that women are socialized to be perfect, to know everything before they take a step. Men are more comfortable making decisions without knowing everything – going on conjecture, projections, or peer-reviews and positivity.

For the Fundraiser and the philanthropic professional women in philanthropy, it is growing and gaining prevalence, confidence, and intentionality. Women are becoming a greater majority of philanthropic leads versus investments. Women in philanthropy is a

---

[29] Lily Family School of Philanthropy, Women's Philanthropy Institute – "First Research in a Decade on Giving Circles."
https://scholarworks.iupui.edu/bitstream/handle/1805/25515/crowdfunding210331-1.pdf?sequence=4&isAllowed=y
[30] "The Impact of Gender on Giving to Crowdfunding Campaigns"
https://philanthropy.iupui.edu/institutes/reseach/gender-crwodfunding.html

clear fit and their expertise through philanthropic investing is a future norm. Many of the old school barriers are coming down, while philanthropic barriers seem to be minimizing – even removed altogether – from woman investing through charitable donations, planned gifts and desired outcomes and NPO mission impacts.

Women are matriculating faster through philanthropic investments versus stock market investments. I believe it is a combination of two distinct skill-set characteristics: (1) Women are gaining more and more confidence in philanthropy's ability, return on charitable investment, and cultural success, whereas (2) men remain private sector myopic, unwilling to research the NPO mission(s), cultural outcomes, and significant impacts, as they do with IPOs, day-trading gamesmanship, and braggadocio of the bull market rewards.

Chapter Eight

The Close

"Donors don't want to become the mercury in some remedial campaign thermometer. That means nothing to them. Donors want impact, purpose, and the pursuit of their personal interests by giving through your mission to produce the outcomes that they so passionate about." – Eric Hogue, Lecture Presentation

In November 2018, I was in Washington, D.C. attending the Trinity Forum Evening Conversation and Senator Ben Sasse from Nebraska was one of the featured speakers discussing the radical changes in our cultural relationships. Senator Sasse argued that, in general, people tend to believe we, as a society, connected more than ever when we aren't really connected at all. Sasse stated, "We are talking at each other with neither side employing any listening." During his 25-minute lecture, the senator made some salient points and I believe they have some merit in the world of philanthropy.

"Our culture has been turned into digital tribes of social media. We are online and in our homes with others who are like-minded, and you step out of line, then you can get voted out of the tribe. These tribes argue with other tribes. We think we are connected to this digital tribe and believe we are communicating, but in reality, we are just talking or arguing and not listening. On the surface, technology looks like it has made our lives better. Instead, it has made our lives, our families and God's purpose for our lives . . . worse."

Senator Sasse continued saying, "We live in a lonely culture. We are hoodwinked by the draw and brand of social media to believe we live in a community, but it is all a lie. Social lives are addicted to the instrument of division and loneliness." I believe the senator to be right on the money. Culture today is divisive, argumentative (without purpose), distanced, and segregated by technological silos and platforms. We are just a shadow of what cultural connectivity represented just fifteen or twenty years ago.

You may wonder what this content has to do with this chapter's title "The Close." Back in the early 2020's, the world went through a 100-year pandemic due to a novel virus called COVID. The pandemic affected all facets of life, culture, political ideology, and economic realities. It also affected philanthropy as we once knew, in particular, my fundraising department at Colorado Christian University.

During the lockdowns and the pandemics high impact months, every aspect of fundraising and our ability to connect with our donors turned to technology and distant relationships through online videos, social media, constant emails, and snail mail. By utilizing Zoom, we thought we were using new technology to build relationships with our donors in a successful way. Just like Senator Sasse said, we were hoodwinked. Real, face-to-face, donor-centric relationships are critical when combined with a listening mechanism.

That is the gold standard of donor-centric fundraising.

The Fundraiser and the donor need to be in dialogue, both verbally and non-verbally, to produce actions and outcomes for the donor's intentional philanthropy. Remember, Fundraising is not friend making, it is an intentional – even professional – trust relationship built over time and in person. As the donor advisor, I need to understand the passion and desires of my donors and their intended support for my NPO.

During the pandemic, webinar after webinar was offered to convince us, the Fundraisers, that technology is just as good – maybe better in the long run – for philanthropy. Let me be very clear, it is a lie and a fallacy. In our anxiety and fear, fundraising joined the social media, technological tribes which offer us nothing but division and no meaningful connectivity. COVID delivered us separation and we fooled ourselves believing we were sincerely cultivating philanthropy when we were just biding time to get to the other side of the pandemic, hungering to reengage with our generous donors. Now that we are mostly on the other side of it, we should understand the success of our NPOs, churches, universities and other charities and ministries is not operated through distant technology, Zoom, or social media. Success comes from connected intentional relationships. As Senator Sasse referred, we have to tell ourselves the truth. Successful cultural connection comes from an old-fashioned method of building a trusted, authentic, relationship.

Senator Sasse made another relevant comment during his lecture: "Our dinner table is in collapse. Jesus drew people to the table where they could eat, to build conversation and community. Today we ignore the table. If we are demanded to sit at the table, we distract and divide our time with our real families. How? We keep our cellphones nearby to monitor our digital platform and tribes." How true this is. As a father, grandfather, and university administrative executive, I am constantly reminded how addicted our culture is to social media and the smart phone technology. I have been encouraged with the "unplug family table baskets" inviting dinner guests to turn off the ringer and place the smart phone into a basket for the duration of dinner and dinner time's valuable discussions. My only dismay is how rapid the younger crowd eats, only to run from the table and return to the controlling device so they can "catch-up on what they missed" over the past hour of dinner time.

The sad part is that this reality is happening across a wide part of our culture, and it is also happening in philanthropic shops for nonprofits. They believe they can build a donor relationship through Zoom, fanciful emails and, distantly, via the menu of internet platforms. I have had to redirect a few MGO appointments from a scheduled Zoom to an airline ticket and personal visit. I love the arguments against, "The airline ticket is costly, I can visit with 4-5 donors in one day versus only one by traveling to them." Or "My donor is a part of the younger generation. They appreciate the Zoom visit as a better option." Again, a technological argument of ease, affordability, and reluctance of sincere donor-centric efforts.

Distanced technological connectivity may help close the ask and receive a gift, but it will not build a sustainable philanthropic relationship. The best donor is the one you have today and not the one you think you are going to get tomorrow. If you retain today's known donor, in five to eight years they may become a major donor and dovetail their giving to different areas in your ministry or nonprofit. They continue to give because they understand their giving has impact because you are personally (with effort) thanking them. You're also going back and giving them a report of the impact and accomplishments. You are listening to them to see if they want to support the impact again or in a different area or at a different level. As the donor's advisor, you build this relationship over time, and donor retention becomes the result. If you connect, you will see valued donors give for five, ten or fifteen years. And these donors will move from $5,000 gifts to a $25,000 gift. Perhaps even a $250,000 cash gift, or legacy planned gift or a gift pledge for $250,000 a year for five years.

Distanced communications and technological platforms do not – please hear me – they do not, will not, produce the substantive relationships and connections you need to be successful for your donor, and successful for the mission of your NPO.

Surveys reveal that donors will stop giving to a university or a church because five percent believed the organization didn't need them anymore. Eight percent stopped because they didn't receive any personal information about how their gifts were used because no one circled back to them. Thirteen percent never received a thank you. Sixteen percent of the donors pass away. Eighteen percent stop because of poor service or poor communication. **Here's the largest most concerning loss of retention statistic:** 36 percent stopped because they believed other missions or nonprofits were more important. In this segmentation of lapsed retention, the donor decides to give somewhere else in hopes of finding a new nonprofit which will develop a relationship with them and even ask them to volunteer at their organization for greater involvement. Stay distanced via technology and you will experience this time and time again. It's best to purchase the airfare, rent the car, stay a night in a hotel, and build a lasting relationship of connectivity versus the sterile and lonely cultivations of smart phones, emails, and online video platforms.

I've lived in five major cities with a local rescue missions that feed, clothe, and shelter homeless individuals. For each of these cities, in the mail, I've received an appeal to give at Thanksgiving and Christmas. For the past 20 years my wife and I give $75 to $100 during the holidays. In time, I received a thank you and a gift receipt letter in response. Yet I have never been called or asked if I, or my family, would like to volunteer at the mission. And I've never been invited to have a one on one conversation about my giving goals. Their appeal is always the same. They ask me to do what I did last year to help feed and clothe the needy people in these cities. When I lived near San Francisco, we donated five $100 gifts to this rescue mission. I provided my phone, email and address each time. It would have been fairly simple for this rescue mission to call me and say, "Next time you are in the city, I'd like to invite you to come by the rescue mission for a cup of coffee and I'll show you what we are doing." If they had made this call, I would have taken an hour, gone to the mission and accepted their tour. I would have met individuals and we would have talked and listened to each other.

If they had made this effort to develop a relationship with me, I would have gone from $100 once or twice a year, to $500/year or

$100 a month. If the mission had cultivated this relationship, reached out to me personally to volunteer, or invited me and my wife to an annual dinner, we would have attended and we would have been connected personally and philanthropically.

Donors do not want to be the red ink in a fundraising thermometer on the stage or to be seen as a gift transaction on Zoom. They want to be known personally as philanthropic investors who are passionate about the outcome of a particular NPO, charity, or vital ministry. If you really want to make "the close," then you have to understand three points about your donors' passions intentionality.

First, you need to know the donor's philanthropic values and desired impacts. This donor may enter your organization with one gift, but they can be retained for fifteen years and give in six or seven different areas.

Second, you want to align the donor's interests within your NPO mission. They may have more than one interest and as you build your relationship, then you will understand how their interests align with your nonprofit. As you listen to these donors, you will understand their interests.

Third, you will want to build a partnership with your donor for the purpose of your NPO mission. If you retain them, then in five, ten, fifteen or twenty years, these individuals will give larger, more defined donations with increased frequency. These donors may even volunteer and recruit other donors for you because they want to help likeminded friends also give to your organization. Through this activity you will grow your roster and soon they will make major donations and pledges. and perhaps even leave a legacy planned gift at the end of their life.

Again, a Zoom session is easy and affordable, and you can "connect" with four to five donors in one day, but none of these three objectives will happen because of an email, a text, a Zoom session, or an online distanced internet-based cultivation event.

As Senator Ben Sasse said, social media looks like we are connected but that is an illusion. Transactional fundraising through technology is raising some dollars, but you are not raising donors, partners, or outcome-based sustainable impact for your NPO or your valuable donor!

At the writing of this book, our country is coming out of a worldwide pandemic, entering a very confusing economy with high inflation, possible recession, and a stock market that is overtly bearish. If you are involved with your donors in a transaction based fundraising relationship, a majority of your donors in your portfolio will stop giving to your organization within the next year. Why? It's simple: The economy will become more concerning to them than your periodic transactional update, ask, or (eventually) plea. But if you build connected donors who partner with your NPO mission, and they feel authentically involved and invested in your NPO, where their gifts are having an impact and bringing about the desired change, you will retain that donor thorough inflation, recession, even a depression. No matter how bad the economy gets, they will never stop giving. They believe in what they are doing AND the role they play in partnering with you for the good of your NPO's mission and outcomes.

When I worked at William Jessup University, we had an annual donor gala where we were very intentional in thanking our prized donors. As we were planning this gala, I asked my team, "Who can we identify from our donor portfolios who has been giving at least $50 a month for over 20 years?"

My Senior Director of Donor Relations at the time, David Pineschi, replied, "We'll find out, Eric."

A few days later, David came to my office and said, "When we did the research, we found this woman in Southern California named Angel, age 88, who has been giving to the university for 40 years at $50 a month."

When I learned about Angel, I said, "Has anyone ever visited with her?"

David shook his head no.

"Why not? Angel obviously believes in William Jessup University and is partnering with WJU's Christ-centered higher education mission. David, I want someone to get on a plane, and go see Angel. Take her to lunch or whatever is most comfortable for her and find out why she gives to William Jessup University."

We sent one of our major gift officers to the Los Angeles area to visit with Angel. The MGO spent the afternoon with Angel and listened to her story. Angel informed us, "I was never allowed to go to college and this lack of education made me bitter. As I grew older, I understood that maybe I wasn't the college type, but I always believed my children and grandchildren should have the opportunity to attend college.

"Because I'm a Christian, I believed my grandchildren could attend a Christian college. When I was living with one of my daughters going through a crisis in Sacramento, I heard about William Jessup University. I decided out of my meager income to give $50 a month and I have been faithfully giving to WJU for fifty years because I believe in what you stand for and offer for college students."

When we heard Angel's story, we invited her to our annual Gala Dinner. Angel was aged, somewhat bent over, struggles to walk at a quick pace and, of course, looked like a loving, aging, grandmother with glasses and gray hair but who lived a life of great purpose. Angel displayed great joy in attending the gala and her demeanor conveyed someone youthfully eager to seize every day.

We seated Angel at my table for the dinner program. That evening we presented Angel with an award in recognition of her faithful giving to the university. After the event, her giving didn't change – we didn't care. Angel lived two more years and passed away at age 90. In her estate was an expressed planned gift to the university of nearly $150,000.

If you remain transactional in how you treat your donors, you will never learn why Angel was giving to the university or what she wanted to do with those funds, such as giving to scholarships. If you accept today's technology as an innovative, timesaving, effort-saving, and budget-saving alternative, you will never build partners, retain partners, and reach the win-win scenarios for your donors and your NPO's vital mission. As Ben Sasse stated, "It a mirage, a lie – real connection never comes through a device."

Some Statistics to Back Up My Information

From a 2018 research study from Indiana University done in partnership with Eli Lilly School of Philanthropy of high-net-worth individuals, the results found 28% of donors stopped giving in 2017 for these three primary reasons: too frequent solicitations (41%, and a sign of transactional fundraising), a belief the organization was not effective or didn't communicate their effectiveness (16%), being asked for an amount from the nonprofit the donor felt was inappropriate. This happens when you are nonprofit centric rather than donor centric in your fundraising practice. You have such a great need that you are asking the donor to satisfy a gap problem, a budget problem or a campaign that is not receiving the right amount of donations.

Donors will desire to help, but in their helping they erode enthusiasm for the NPO and the optimism in future outcomes. You know the donor could afford to give $10,000 but, due to the frenetic urgency, you are asking for $50,000. Your motivation as the Fundraiser is to get the dollars rather than advise the donor in relationship to their intentions, passions, and desired outcomes. When you make this grave mistake, you are sending a red flare to your donor through a very insensitive request. Most donors will laugh when you make that outrageous ask and become immediately put off, "I know you have this great need, but I do not have that amount of money to give you at this time and I'm offended that you think I do."

In times of urgent CEO/Director fundraising requests, you must remain loyal to a donor-centric process and focused relationship. This is vital because when you have invested time and relational capital to develop a sincere donor relationship, you will know how much you can ask in times of crisis or NPO necessity. You will also know if you should NOT offer a request of donation from particular donors. Your word to your CEO or director needs to represent your donor portfolio and not the pleas of the organization, or its executive leadership.

Create rules for your work as an MGO, guidelines and boundaries. It's perfectly fine to report to your supervisor that your donor(s) are not cultivated, prepared, or desiring to participate in crisis campaigns. In 2002 Rick Warren wrote *The Purpose Driven Life* with five major points. Warren's results in writing this book became epic, in and outside of the church. I've taken the great liberty in modifying these points for my department and label the five points below as "purpose driven philanthropy:"

1. You must plan for the donor's pleasure.

2. You must form everything you do for the donor's passions.

3. You must create impact with the donor's donations.

4. You must shape outcomes with the donor's donations.

5. You must commit and make the relationship sustainable over time.

What do the donors think?

Lisa Greer who is a major donor herself, has written a book about how the donor process needs to be improved. As she has worked with major gift officers who have built relationships with her and then asked for a donation for their nonprofit, Lisa said, "Seeing our money help others, has been one of the greatest joys of my life. Often, I get to be living proof of the studies that tout the physical and psychological benefits of giving for the giver."[31] The Bible tells us that God desires for us to be a cheerful giver and, in most cases, when you do give, you are immediately cheerful. Giving does produce a physical adrenaline satisfaction and a psychological benefit for the giver of the gift.[32] It's how God has made us. You can have a joy-filled life as a giver.

Lisa's comment goes to the heart of the donor-centric process. "Fundraisers need to understand that it is not just about the donor or the nonprofit organization. It is about the origin of life itself when we give to others, we give for impact or outcome for God's glory to help cure a disease or provide the means for someone to walk, or of someone to see, or someone who has no food to eat, or a place to live, there is a God-created satisfaction to that."[33] When we don't operate in a donor-centric fashion and instead operate in a transactional manner, we take that satisfaction and joy away from the giver because we make it a business deal or a sales deal of a simple transaction.

Lisa continues, "I'm convinced people aren't giving as much because the process of giving is fundamentally flawed. If today's fundraising tactics actually preclude connection instead of fostering it, will people continue to give?"[34] There is a donor's passion, a donor's

---

[31] Greer, *Philanthropy Revolution*, 33.
[32] Bible, 2 Corinthians 9:6-7.
[33] Greer, *Philanthropy Revolution*, 36.
[34] Greer, *Philanthropy Revolution*, 29.

heart, a donor's psyche and a donor's mindset which needs to be understood in order to not steal the psychological blessing.

The Wrap for The Call

I'm currently working with a donor who is nearly ninety years of age. He was a major donor to Colorado Christian University before I came and has continued giving to the university in the five years since I've been the Vice President of Advancement at CCU. When I say major, this generous donor has given a number of multi-million-dollar gifts. He is battling some health issues which he does not like to talk about or discuss. I frequently visit with him in his office (he makes some terrible Sanka-like coffee for us to sip from during our visits). Each time we get together, I joke, "Ben, I love you, but I hate your coffee." Yet when we meet, he will make a cup for himself and one for me. I will drink as many sips and swigs as I can handle, and he laughs every time.

Recently Ben informed me, "Eric, in the four and a half years you have been here at Colorado Christian University, I've enjoyed our time together drinking bad coffee and talking about my gifts to the university. You send handwritten thank you cards, and you call me on the phone to tell me how my gifts to the scholarship fund produced these three students who are doing well in their studies. Thank you for doing that so regularly – it's a real joy to receive your updates. I also appreciate the questions you've asked about legacy gifts and I understand why you are asking. I want you to know I am not offended when you ask. I'm actually thankful when you do because it is not just about my donation but my end-of-life plans before the Lord."

"I have enjoyed our numerous conversations about what heaven will be like and what my kids and grandkids will go through with my passing. You've been reassuring, encouraging and you have listened to me – even tried to answer my silly questions. But I need to tell you one thing."

"Ben, what's that?"

"I'm not going to leave a legacy gift to the university because I'm going to spend it all now so I can enjoy it before I get to heaven." Then Ben gave me a check for a few million dollars for the university.

"When you circle back around, there will be a few more gifts, but there will not be a legacy gift because I want to watch and see what happens. I want you to call me and tell me the impact. I know I will be thankful to give God the glory and praise for the outcome and rejoice with you."

When I left our time together and sat in the driver's seat of my car – in an attempt to complete a contact report, I was overtaken by the encounter and Ben's amazing generosity. I grew thankful for Ben, the role I play for the university, and the opportunities to be impacted by so many silent heroes of philanthropy.

I want to be very clear, this experience with Ben did not come about because of an email, a text, or a Zoom call. Sarcastically, you can't taste the bad Sanka on Zoom. It developed because of an intentional donor-centric relationship with a very generous donor named Ben. We meet with authenticity, clear intentionality and complete transparency about what He wants to do through CCU for the income and outcome that God has placed on his investment philanthropy.

If you are a novice or seasoned Fundraiser, there will be times that you make a mistake and become transactional in your donor relations. If you can, immediately go back and fix it and promise yourself to never, willingly, do it again! There is a joy to this job which is unexplainable. When you are a Fundraiser and focused on the donor, it is not about you, or your nonprofit, it is the joy of the journey of the donor and what he or she wants to do with his or her giving. When you have constructed this type of donor relationship over time and become a trusted donor advisor, Fundraising is no longer a job, it is an honorable vocation, service, and ministry for the donor and the NPO alike.

In as much as the donor feels the euphoric joy of making a major donation, as the Fundraiser, you also feel this same endorsement of joy and satisfaction. Such an experience is so anti-cultural, you can actually feel God's endorsement and satisfaction In the end, you will build your fundraising success from *the winning side of the ask.*

Acknowledgements

It takes a number of good people to make a 'rookie writer' make sense on the written page. I want to acknowledge and thank a few key performers in this project.

Terry Wahlin for his constant patience in listening to me talk incessantly about "donor-centric fundraising." Terry's writing expertise brings to life each donor story and philanthropic episode in this book.

Greg Johnson, my literary agent. Greg's gentle professional guidance throughout the publishing process has been a gift. He deserves a high honor for his attentive mentoring of this first time, novice, author.

Lance Oversole, a close friend, former CCU colleague, and "comms master" who gave of his time and talent to edit my run on sentences, poor adjectives, and fragmented sentence.

Kiersti Torok, our oldest daughter and the family's first author. Kiersti's encouragement was my fuel to write, publish and push through. In reality, both of our daughters, Kiersti and our youngest, **Kourtnee Lasick**, are constant encouragers and "daddy cheerleaders." I am a blessed father!

My **Professional Colleagues** at William Jessup University and Colorado Christian University, you experienced a good portion of this book's successes, the lessons learned (good and bad), and each philanthropic experiment. Thank you for your commitment to excellence, professionalism, and my leadership; I'm forever thankful. Christ-centered Higher Education, for your distinct and compelling liberal arts, humanities, biblically integrated pedagogy, and your eternal significance for each and every student enrolled at your institution(s).

May **Christ-centered education** be forever committed to Jesus, God's Holy Word, the sincere and liberating pursuit of truth, all-the-while being full of God's love and grace, shown through Jesus His Son, our Savior, for the salvation of mankind.

About Eric K. Hogue

Eric Hogue joined Colorado Christian University as the vice president of Advancement in January 2018. He oversees all University fundraising efforts including campaigns for annual, capital, endowment, planned gifts, alumni, parents, and athletics.

Hogue has overhauled the University's fundraising systems and processes with the goal of creating a diversified donor-centric philanthropic operation staffed by experienced professionals. His current focus is completing the campaign for the Science Center and growing the University endowment to $100 million.

Prior to joining CCU, Hogue served for six years as the chief development officer (CDO) of William Jessup University in Rocklin, California, where he successfully tripled WJU's endowment fund and navigated two separate and successful campus capital development campaigns. He is also known for his roles as a former political candidate; practicing theologian and pastor; and long-tenured radio, television, and media professional.

Hogue enjoys stewarding relationships toward biblical generosity for Christ-centered higher education. His hobbies include watching sports and documentaries, reading good books, cooking, and running. Hogue has been married to Tammy Hogue for more than three decades and together they are the parents of two wonderful adult daughters, two amazing sons-in-law, and three brilliant grandchildren.

HOGUE PHILANTHROPIC SOLUTIONS, LLC.

Thank you for reading this book. I'm available for workshops, fundraising conference, and consulting opportunities:

- Annual Campaign Strategies
- Major Gifts Training
- Capital Campaign Feasibility and Design
- Planned Gift Cultivation and Vehicles
- Endowment Growth Campaigns
- Professional Portfolio Management
- Organizational Management and Design
- Communications and Marketing
- Board Presentations
- Strategic Planning Retreats
- Executive Coaching

HPS.

Hogue Philanthropic Solutions, LLC

"Donor-centric Philosophies for a Better World and Better Results"

Eric Hogue, Principal Owner

(916) 276-4676

eric@hoguephilanthropic.com

www.kudzucourses.com

Kudzu Courses are a series of <u>on-demand, online video courses,</u> designed for **Fundraisers like just you**. Learn tactical strategies and hear big ideas from experienced fundraising professional **Eric Hogue**. **Kudzu Courses** will equip you with the skills, tools, and donor-centric strategies you need to *<u>grow your success philanthropy overnight</u>*.

Kudzu Courses are affordable online courses that deliver <u>relevant training and logistical instruction</u> for today's fundraising professional. Unlike expensive, time consuming, travel demanding national conferences and seminars, **Kudzu Courses** deliver the immediate expertise you need to grow your fundraising overnight.

"Kudzu Comes to You!"

ENDNOTES

Introduction

1 Lisa Greer, *Philanthropy Revolution* (London: Harper Collins, 2020), 48.

Chapter One

2 Jim Langley, *The Future of Fundraising* (Denver, Colorado: Academic Impressions Publishers, 2020), 5.

3 Mark Dillon, *Giving and Getting in the Kingdom of God* (Chicago, Illinois: Moody Press, 2012), 41.

4 Dillon, *Giving and Getting in the Kingdom of God*, 37.

Chapter Two

5 Lynne Wester, *The Four Pillars of Donor Relations* (Denver, Colorado: Academic Impressions, 2019), 18.

6 Greer, *Philanthropy Revolution*, 27.

Chapter Three

7 Roger M. Craver, *Retention Fundraising* (Medfield, Massachusetts: Emerson & Church, 2014), 29.

Chapter Four

8 Doris Kearns, *Team of Rivals* (New York, NY: Simon & Schuster, 2005), 47.

9 Jason McNeal, Ph.D., *Writing Meaningful Contact Reports: A Handbook for Fundraisers* (Academic Impressions, Denver, CO., 2019), a very useful book for contact report building.

10 Russ Alan Prince and Karen Maru File, *The Seven Faces of Philanthropy* (Jossey-Bass Publishers, San Francisco, CA., 1994), 13-17.

11 Greer, *Philanthropy Revolution*, 56.

12 *Crowdfunding the New Testament*, WSJ, November 27, 2021.

Chapter Five

13 Joseph Tumolo, *Go See People Grow Your Fundraising Program,* 67-69.

14 James M. Langley, *The Future of Fundraising,* 51-55.

15 Dan Pallotta, *The Way We Think About Charity is Dead Wrong*, YouTube, TED Talk, February 2013.

16 Joseph Tumolo, *Go See People Grow Your Fundraising Program,* 23-27.

Chapter Six

17 Deborah Grayson Reigel, *Why the Most Successful Leaders Don't Care About Being Liked, https://www.inc.com/deborah-grayson-riegel/why-most-successful-leaders-dont-care-about-being-liked.html* (Inc. Magazine, 2019).

18 Jim Collins, *Good to Great* (New York, NY: HarperCollins, 2001), 1.

19 Croteau and Smith, Making the Case for Leadership, 115.

20 Ibid, 121-122.

21 Ibid, 125.

22 Ibid, 147.

23 Ibid, 216.

24 Ibid, 21.

25 Croteau and Smith, Making the Case for Leadership, 191-200.

Chapter Seven

26 Mark Dillon, *Giving & Getting in the Kingdom,* 63.

27 Lisa Greer, *Philanthropy Revolution*, 88.

28 Lily Family School of Philanthropy, Women's Philanthropy Institute – *"First Research in a Decade on Giving Circles."* https://scholarworks,iupui.edu/bitstream/handle/1805/25515/crowdfu nding210331-1.pdf?sequence=4&isAllowed=y

29 Lily Family School of Philanthropy, *"The Impact of Gender on Giving to Crowdfunding Campaigns"* https://philanthropy.iupui.edu/institutes/reseach/gender-crwodfunding.html

Chapter Eight

30 Greer, *Philanthropy Revolution*, 33.

31 Bible, 2 Corinthians 9:6-7.

32 Greer, *Philanthropy Revolution*, 36.

33 Ibid, 29.

Made in the USA
Monee, IL
25 May 2023

34572225R00134